CAREERS WITHOUT COLLEGE

FITNESS

**Other titles in
this series include:**

CARS
COMPUTERS
FASHION
HEALTH CARE
MUSIC

FITNESS

by Maura Rhodes Curless

Series developed by Peggy Schmidt

Peterson's

Princeton, New Jersey

A New Century Communications Book

Curless, Maura Rhodes, 1959–
    Fitness / by Maura Rhodes Curless.
        p.   cm.—(Careers without college)
    "A New Century Communications book."
    Includes bibliographical references.
    ISBN 1-56079-223-X : $7.95
    1. Physical fitness—Vocational guidance—United States.
I. Title.   II. Series.
GV510.U5C87   1992
613.7′0973—dc20   92-31182
                                                                          CIP

Art direction: Linda Huber
Cover and interior design: Greg Wozney Design, Inc.
Cover photo: Bryce Flynn Photography
Composition: Bookworks Plus
Printed in the United States of America
10 9 8 7 6 5

Text Photo Credits
Color photo graphics: J. Gerard Smith Photography
Page xiv: © Woodfin Camp & Associates, Inc./Lester Sloan
Page 18: © Woodfin Camp & Associates, Inc./William Strode
Page 36: © Black Star/Bob Krist
Page 54: © Bruce Curtis
Page 70: © Woodfin Camp & Associates, Inc./Leif Skoogfors

ABOUT THIS SERIES

Careers without College is designed to help those who don't have a four-year college degree (and don't plan on getting one any time soon) find a career that fits their interests, talents and personalities. It's for you if you're about to choose your career—or if you're planning to change careers and don't want to invest a lot of time or money in more education or training, at least not right at the start.

Some of the jobs featured do require an associate degree; others only require on-the-job training that may take a year, some months or only a few weeks. In today's real world, with its increasingly competitive job market, you may want to eventually consider getting a two- or maybe a four-year college degree in order to move up in the world.

Careers without College has up-to-date information that comes from extensive interviews with experts in each field. It's fresh, it's exciting, and it's easy to read. Plus, each book gives you something unique: an insider look at the featured jobs through interviews with people who work in them now.

Peggy Schmidt

ACKNOWLEDGEMENTS

Special thanks to the fitness professionals who dedicated their time, energy and expertise to providing information for this book.

Douglas Brooks, M.S., Personal Trainer and Adviser, IDEA: The Association for Fitness Professionals

Joe Cerulli, Owner, Gainesville Health and Fitness Center, Gainesville, Florida

Anthony Cortes, Personal Trainer, Los Angeles, California

Kathie Davis, Founder and Executive Director, IDEA: The Association for Fitness Professionals

Amy DeGroot, Director of Communications, American Council on Exercise (ACE)

Jocelyn Granger, Sports Massage Therapist, Ann Arbor Therapeutic Massage Clinic, Ann Arbor, Michigan

Susan Johnson, Ed.D., Associate Director of Continuing Education and Consulting, Cooper Institute for Aerobics Research, Dallas, Texas

Julie Laria, Marketing Assistant, Jazzercize, Inc.

Dawn Norman, M. A., General Manager, Multiplex Health Club, Deerfield, Illinois

Ruth Sova, President and Founder, Aquatic Exercise Association

Ralph Stevens, Owner, Helping Hands Body Therapy Center, Iowa City, Iowa

Claudia Westcott, Fitness Director, South Shore YMCA, Boston, Massachusetts

Jennifer Jo Wilson, Director of Communications, IDEA: The Association for Fitness Professionals

Thanks also to Carol Mauro for her editing expertise.

WHAT'S IN THIS BOOK

WHY THESE FITNESS CAREERS?

People who pursue fitness careers usually love working out and being where the action is—in a health club, an aerobics studio, a YMCA or a resort. If that description fits you, you may decide you would like to be the one leading the aerobics class, taking a client through the paces of a one-on-one workout or selling health club memberships. The good news is that it is possible to find just the right career to feed your personal passion for fitness. This book discusses in detail five choices:

❑ Group exercise instructor

❑ Sports massage therapist

❑ Sales and service staff

❑ Personal trainer

❑ Floor staff

These careers were chosen because a four-year college education is not required to get into them. Employers are usually more impressed by characteristics that cannot be learned from a book: enthusiasm, a natural talent for leading and teaching, an outgoing and friendly personality, patience and a commitment to health and fitness. If you have your sights set on a job that involves working directly with exercisers, however, you should go through a training and certification program at a nationally recognized fitness organization.

The three careers that involve working directly with exercisers—group exercise instructor, personal trainer and floor staffer—require many of the same skills and fitness know-how. How you put your expertise to work varies greatly in each of these jobs, however. Group exercise instructors, for example, must be comfortable working in front of and with a group of people, have a teacher's mindset and an ear for music. Group communication skills are not important for personal trainers because they work one-on-one with clients, but because they are often self-employed, trainers do need to know how to get and keep clients. Floor staffers are like lifeguards: They need a keen eye to make sure exercisers are using equipment properly and using correct exercise form, and they need the diplomacy to show them how if they're not.

Working in the fitness field can be physically demanding and mentally challenging. You will be in constant motion, whether you're leading a class or watching over a room full of people lifting weights. You will need to keep up with the latest research about fitness by reading journals, and you will be expected to stay on top of new training techniques by attending lectures, workshops and continuing education courses. But because each person you deal with is different, and because fitness is changing all the time, you will rarely have a dull moment. Sometimes the work is hard and the pay is low, but if you are dedicated and persevere, you can do well. As proof, at the end of each chapter you will find three interviews with people who have pursued a career in fitness without the benefit of a four-year college degree—and have succeeded.

Besides these success stories, Judi Sheppard Missett, the founder and president of Jazzercise, offers interesting insight into career opportunities in fitness. Also, three famous people tell about their humble beginnings: top New York aerobics studio owner, Jeff Martin; the creator of step training, Gin Miller; and Robert DeNiro's personal trainer of eight years, Dan Harvey.

JUDI SHEPPARD MISSETT

on Why Now Is the Right Time for a Fitness Career

Judi Sheppard Missett, the founder and president of Jazzercise, is a pioneer in the field of fitness. She was the first to marry music and exercise—long before aerobic dancers started bobbing to pop. A dancer from childhood, Missett was performing and teaching jazz in Evanston, Illinois, when she noticed that many of her students were routinely dropping out after a few lessons. They did not seem interested in the professional dance training they were being offered. The aspirations of these women, mostly housewives and college students, were not to the stage but to trimmer bodies and a desire to have fun.

Missett decided there needed to be an exercise alternative to dance classes and the main other fitness class choice at the time, calisthenics. She created Jazzercise, a fitness routine that was fun and performed to music, and then she got the word out and taught the first class to 15 people in 1969. By the second class that number had doubled; 22 years later, more than 400,000 fitness enthusiasts burn calories and tone up their bodies regularly with Jazzercise.

Current classes are taught by instructors who buy a Jazzercise franchise after going through a thorough training program. Missett's passion for her work and her good common sense have nurtured her company into one of the top-ranked franchise operations in the world. Missett herself has a gold record, two gold videotapes, a best-selling book and a successful mail-order fitness gear business.

Although Jazzercise has evolved into big business, Missett remains closely involved: She single handedly choreographs the 30 new routines that are videotaped and sent out to instructors worldwide every eight months, and she teaches five classes a week herself. This dedication to her company, along with Jazzercise's longevity, gives Missett a unique vantage point from which to observe the fitness field. She was there when the fitness boom began, and she has watched the industry grow. Here's what she has to say about career opportunities in the fitness field and what it takes to get started—and to get ahead.

The wonderful thing about working in the fitness industry right now is that the field is still in its infancy. There are all sorts of exciting avenues to explore as it evolves. We know what makes people fit, but only ten percent of the population does any sort of regular exercise. That leaves a lot of people who need to be motivated to get into shape; as new ways are created to inspire the couch potatoes, new career options develop.

Research is also expanding the career choices for fitness enthusiasts: We have so many scientists out there studying how the body works, how it responds to different types of activity and how it can be improved; I think we've only seen the tip of the iceberg. As new insights into fitness and health emerge, so do new exercise disciplines that may open more career doors.

I think that the fitness industry is going the way of the medical profession in that more and more fitness professionals are specializing in distinct populations of people— for example, teaching aerobics classes for kids and doing personal training with adults who have disabilities. If you pursue a career in fitness, you may be able to carve your own niche of expertise.

I find that this industry is also one of the most gratifying to work in. It provides a wonderful opportunity for self-expression. Aerobics teachers must choreograph new routines, and personal trainers and health club staffers are constantly being met with challenges that require them to be creative.

What's more, you can see your students or clients change right before your eyes, both physically and emotionally. I have been motivated to work hard at making Jazzercise successful by my students and their reactions to what I do. Frequently students tell me that taking Jazzercise classes helped them get through a family death or gave them the confidence to move into a new career or the strength to endure a painful divorce. These stories have been a primary source of inspiration for me.

I don't feel that four years of college is absolutely necessary to succeed at the five careers discussed in this book. When we hire people at Jazzercise, we don't always look for that degree. There are other traits that are more essential to success and that just can't be picked up from a college professor.

First and foremost, you must be passionate about what you're doing—whether you're leading a large group of people through a step class or massaging the kinks out of an individual's body. Out of passion develops a strong work ethic, and without that you won't succeed. Some people go into fitness careers thinking, "Oh, it will be a nice thing to do and it will keep me fit, too." These people don't survive because they don't have enough dedication.

You must also have the kind of personality that attracts people—you have to be enthusiastic and positive—and you must be giving of yourself. At the same time, you have to be giving *to* yourself and realize that you need to give yourself down time, because this profession is both physically and emotionally draining. It is very easy to get burned out, so you need to be able to balance your business life with your personal life. If you go overboard in one area, the other will suffer.

I would say, too, that it's really important to have a lot of common sense and street sense, particularly if you aspire to own your own business. Jazzercise grew because I listened to what I call "cues," gut feelings. In 1974, I copyrighted the name of my company for no other reason than because a little voice told me it would be a smart idea. Since then, I've had to defend my claim to the Jazzercise name—and I've won. When videocassette recorders came out in the late seventies, my instincts told me that I should take advantage of this new technology: I had been writing out the steps to the routines I sent my instructors; with the VCR I was able to record videos of the new choreographies so they could be easily translated and safely and effectively taught.

Truly good fitness professionals are risk takers. The still-evolving nature of the field dictates that those who work in it be willing to try new things. This is an industry that changes constantly. You have to be open to change and look on it as an opportunity to grow. If you can't do that, if change frightens you or annoys you because it upsets the status quo, then this probably isn't the field for you.

There's no doubt about it, this is a fabulous time to pursue a career in fitness: The industry has developed solid standards and guidelines, yet there is still a great opportunity to develop your own style and perhaps hit on the fitness routine that will get some of those nonexercisers moving. One of the best things about working in this field is that you will be surrounded by other people who share your enthusiasm for health, fitness and nutrition. They will be open minded and forward thinking and have a positive approach to their work and their lives. And that can be a heck of a lot of fun.

FAMOUS BEGINNINGS

Gin Miller, Creator of Step Reebok

Gin Miller was an exercise instructor in Atlanta when she injured her knee. She strengthened her leg by stepping up and down a porch step. She soon realized she had stepped right into a gold mine: a new way to get a cardiovascular workout. She had steps built for her own classes, and when a Reebok rep proclaimed it a hot idea, Miller had an exercise physiologist test her workout for effectiveness and safety. Now Miller's brainchild is famous all over the country, and it has created an industry that includes step training shoes, clothing and videotapes.

Jeff Martin, Owner of Jeff Martin Studio, New York

When Jeff Martin, an overweight, aspiring actor, landed a role that required him to remove his shirt, his flabby physique lost him the part. The next day he started taking dance lessons and running. Then he began teaching jazz dance to some friends in a rented rehearsal space. He got to be so successful that people like Barbara Walters and Joan Lunden started dropping by to exercise. From there Martin's business took off. Now he teaches all over the world, choreographs videos and keeps a lot of New Yorkers in tip-top shape.

Dan Harvey, Robert DeNiro's Personal Trainer

Dan Harvey set out to make his fortune as a model, and to stay in great shape he began working out at a Manhattan health club. To earn his keep he did informal training with a few of the members. His unique exercise style caught the eye of the management, and pretty soon he was getting celebrity clients. Actor Robert DeNiro was so impressed by Harvey that he hired him to be his personal trainer. Eight years later Harvey works regularly with DeNiro and even travels with the actor to movie locations all over the world.

Group exercise instructors have rhythm and an ear for dance music. They know a *lot* about the body and the principles of effective exercise. They know all the right moves, avoiding steps and exercises that can be harmful. Because their students come to them with questions about weight loss and muscle aches and pains, they need to be familiar with the basics of nutrition and sports medicine.

The most successful instructors generally have a broad range of exercises they can teach. That's because although traditional aerobic dance is still quite popular, it has given birth to a whole new generation of exercise options—from low-impact aerobics to step training, from Jazzercise to aquatic workouts. Some exercise variations don't focus on aerobic fitness at all, such as stretch classes, muscle-sculpting workouts and circuit training, in which exercisers do a series of strength-building moves in a particular order.

As a group exercise instructor, you can take your knowledge and skills to a variety of places. You might choose to work only for an aerobics studio, where besides teaching you might assist at the front desk. Or you might freelance, bringing your personal style of instruction to health clubs, YMCAs, recreation centers, aerobics studios and the like. Some group exercise teachers who are employed by health clubs not only lead classes but also help to oversee the weight room. Instructors may conduct classes for such special groups as children, pregnant women and senior citizens.

Wherever and whomever a group exercise instructor chooses to teach, he or she probably will not be able to make a full-time job of it. Because leading fitness classes is so strenuous, those who do it usually limit themselves to no more than two classes a day, to avoid injury and burnout. For this reason, teaching exercise is often a sideline for many people. On the other hand, group instructors are finding ways to increase their income by also doing personal training and leading workshops. Those with a head for business may open their own studios.

A group exercise instructor needs to feel comfortable leading groups of people. He or she will have to move easily and keep abreast of the latest steps and aerobic exercise trends. Above all, if you choose to become a group instructor, you'll need to keep your students hooked on fitness by making your classes fun. And that means having a good time yourself.

What You Need to Know:

- ❑ Anatomy (where muscles, bones and joints are located and what they do)
- ❑ Kinesiology (how the body moves)
- ❑ Exercise physiology (how the body responds to exercise)
- ❑ Principles of exercise (how to put together safe routines that produce good results)
- ❑ Basic nutrition (the basic food groups and what makes up a high-energy, balanced diet)
- ❑ How to prevent and treat exercise-related injuries
- ❑ A variety of safe, effective aerobic exercise moves
- ❑ How to choose music of the correct rhythm for the different stages of an aerobic workout
- ❑ How to choreograph an exercise/dance routine

Necessary Skills

- ❑ Ability to lead and motivate a group of people through a workout
- ❑ An eyes-in-the-back-of-the-head knack for observing many exercisers at once
- ❑ Ability to break down steps into easy-to-follow segments
- ❑ Cueing (giving exercisers well-timed directions for changes in steps so they can follow the routine easily)

Do You Have What It Takes?

- ❑ Tactfulness (when it is necessary to correct a class participant in front of everyone)
- ❑ Coordination and a keen sense of rhythm
- ❑ An enthusiastic, motivating personality
- ❑ Patience
- ❑ A desire to teach and see people improve

Physical Attributes

- ❑ Being in such good physical condition that you can endure long periods of exercise

❏ Nonsmoker

Education

A high school diploma is helpful but not necessary.

Licenses Required

Increasingly, group exercise instructors are expected by employers to be certified by such professional organizations as the American Council on Exercise (ACE), the Aerobics and Fitness Association of America (AFAA) or the Cooper Institute for Aerobics Research. Jazzercise instructors must be trained and certified by Jazzercise, Inc. Certification in cardiopulmonary resuscitation (CPR, a set of skills used when someone has stopped breathing or his or her heart has stopped) is also often required.

Job Outlook

Competition for jobs: somewhat competitive

As public interest in fitness continues to grow, the demand for good exercise instructors will also grow. This is true especially at health clubs, which must offer a wide variety of classes to appeal to as many members as possible. Since fitness is a popular career choice, however, opportunities are limited to the most qualified.

The Ground Floor

Entry-level job: group exercise instructor

This position is usually a part-time one since it is physically impossible to teach classes 40 hours a week. You may, however, combine this job with other responsibilities in a fitness center, including working at the front desk or on the weight room floor, to fill in the hours as well as the dollars.

On-the-Job Responsibilities

Beginners (who teach in aerobics studios or at health clubs, YMCAs and other fitness facilities):

❏ Select appropriate music for each segment of a workout (energizing for the warm-up, relaxing for stretching, etc.)

❑ Create safe, effective exercise routines geared toward the fitness level of the class (for example, beginner versus advanced)

❑ Be vigilant about class safety (make sure exercise space is not overcrowded; that participants are wearing proper shoes; that exercisers with special needs, such as pregnant women, are in the appropriate class)

❑ Take the class through the entire workout

❑ Be on hand afterward to answer questions, demonstrate complicated steps, etc.

Advanced (manager of an aerobics studio or director of a health club aerobics program):

❑ Make up schedules for many different classes

❑ Coordinate instructors and their teaching times

❑ Take care of money matters (collect per-class payments, for instance)

❑ Open and close studio

Your work hours will revolve around when members have time for fitness routines. The most popular times for classes for most working people are in the morning between 6 and 10 A.M., lunchtime, and from around 4:30 P.M. into the early evening. Weekends are also popular work-out times.

◆ **When You'll Work**

Unless you are the manager of a studio or the aerobics director at a health club, you will probably work part time. Four or five classes a week is an average part-time teaching load.

◆ **Time Off**

❑ The chance to maintain your own fitness while you work

❑ If you are employed by a club, full use of club facilities (equipment, sauna, pool); discounts on club amenities (massage, pro shop purchases); and lowered membership rates for immediate family

◆ **Perks**

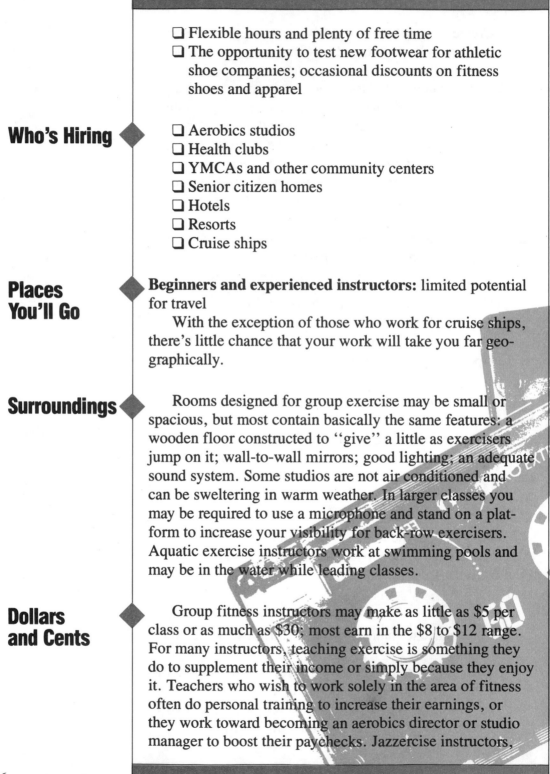

❏ Flexible hours and plenty of free time
❏ The opportunity to test new footwear for athletic shoe companies; occasional discounts on fitness shoes and apparel

Who's Hiring

❏ Aerobics studios
❏ Health clubs
❏ YMCAs and other community centers
❏ Senior citizen homes
❏ Hotels
❏ Resorts
❏ Cruise ships

Places You'll Go

Beginners and experienced instructors: limited potential for travel

With the exception of those who work for cruise ships, there's little chance that your work will take you far geographically.

Surroundings

Rooms designed for group exercise may be small or spacious, but most contain basically the same features: a wooden floor constructed to "give" a little as exercisers jump on it; wall-to-wall mirrors; good lighting; an adequate sound system. Some studios are not air conditioned and can be sweltering in warm weather. In larger classes you may be required to use a microphone and stand on a platform to increase your visibility for back-row exercisers. Aquatic exercise instructors work at swimming pools and may be in the water while leading classes.

Dollars and Cents

Group fitness instructors may make as little as $5 per class or as much as $30; most earn in the $8 to $12 range. For many instructors, teaching exercise is something they do to supplement their income or simply because they enjoy it. Teachers who wish to work solely in the area of fitness often do personal training to increase their earnings, or they work toward becoming an aerobics director or studio manager to boost their paychecks. Jazzercise instructors, who buy a franchise from the corporation (which gives them the right to use the Jazzercise name if they follow certain rules), run their businesses independently and can gross as much as $85,000 a year.

Teachers who remain at one location, say a club or a studio, and perform consistently well may eventually be promoted to a manager position. Otherwise there is no official way to move up in the group exercise field. Your degree of success is determined by demand: If you are repeatedly asked to teach at different clubs and studios and have a faithful group of exercisers who go out of their way to take your class wherever and whenever you teach, then you've made it.

◆**Moving Up**

The most prestigious and better-paying exercise studios are located in New York and Los Angeles. However, nearly every city and town in the U.S. has at least one health club, aerobics facility, YMCA or YWCA—and a need for qualified teachers.

◆**Where the Jobs Are**

There are dozens of small certification programs and workshops run by professional and industry associations. Two of the most widely recognized are: the American Council on Exercise (ACE) and the Aerobics and Fitness Association of America (AFAA). Both offer workshops in the basics of anatomy, kinesiology (how the body moves), exercise physiology and other fitness subjects.

◆**Training**

It is estimated that 90 percent of all group exercise instructors are women. However, most employers welcome men to lead some of the classes and to help draw a male clientele.

◆**The Male/Female Equation**

Making Your Decision: What to Consider

◆ The Bad News

❑ Earnings are low
❑ Physical demands limit number of teaching hours
❑ No formal career ladder
❑ Potential for injury from too heavy a teaching schedule

The Good News

❑ Many part-time job opportunities
❑ Flexible scheduling
❑ For the highly motivated, opportunities to manage or own studios or direct the aerobics programs at health clubs
❑ Job allows you to stay in top physical condition

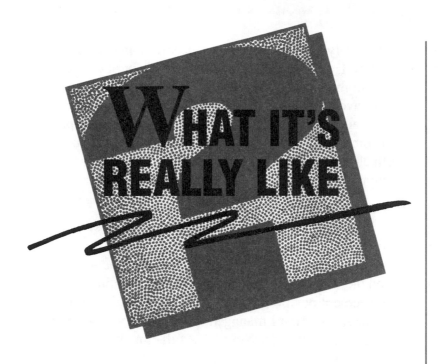

Stacey Fornabaio, 27, exercise instructor
and manager,
Bourne Exercise Studio,
Scarsdale, New York
Years in the business: eight

What do you do in your job?
I manage the studio, teach classes and train instructors.

How did you break in?
I've danced since I was six or seven years old. As I grew
older, I wanted a job that was somehow related to my dance
experience, and that's what led me into fitness. My first
position was as a fitness instructor and aerobics teacher at a
women's health club; I was trained by the manager of that
club.

What did you do there?
I taught exercise classes, and I also designed programs for
people who were using Universal machines. I worked
maybe three nights a week.

How long were you at that health club?
I stayed about six months, then I decided it was time to

9

move on. My next job was very similar, at an exercise studio where I was trained by the director. I taught classes several nights a week for only about six months as well. In fact, I stayed briefly at all the jobs that led to my present one, because I felt that once I learned enough at one place, it was time to go someplace else. I worked at a few other health clubs, too, where I mostly taught and was trained by different directors.

How did you land a job as a studio manager?
After I had been teaching for about four years, I started wanting to grow more in the profession. Since just teaching classes was financially not going to cut it for me and since I loved the field so much, I decided to become involved in a management position. I came to Bourne Studio to train as the manager. At first I managed only part time during evenings and on weekends. Now it's a full-time thing, 30 to 40 hours a week.

What does your job involve?
I teach about six classes a week. In between, I do all the paperwork for the studio, keeping track of billing and memberships and setting up instructors' schedules. I try to keep members happy and satisfied with our services. I try to sell memberships to new people. When a new instructor is hired, I teach her how to teach exercise—the elements of a class, how it should be structured, how to match the music to movement, how to cue for changes in the exercise routine and how to choreograph each routine.

Did you encounter any roadblocks when you started out as a manager?
I've always struggled a bit with getting instructors to respect me, since all of them here are older than I am. It's been a problem, and there's always been some tension.

What do you like most about what you're doing now?
The level of professionalism at this studio is fantastic, and I was looking for that. In fact I was overwhelmed by it when I first came here, since I didn't see this kind of professional teaching in health clubs. I like the small size of this studio, too, and that those of us working here can get to know everyone and offer our expertise to everybody. But the thing I love most about my job—even though I'm a

manager—is teaching. It's what brought me to fitness in the first place.

Besides having to overcome being younger than those you manage, is there anything else you can do without?
Not really. As with any service business, you always have to deal with difficult people, but I don't have a lot of that. And I don't mind the paperwork either because I've always been a very organized person.

What advice do you have for someone who wishes to make a career of fitness, as you've done?
Certification is really important, but you have to be able to teach a class first. One way to learn is to get involved as a student. Then find a mentor, someone to train you. If I were considering someone for a job as an instructor, the first thing I would have her do is teach a trial class. If she was good, I would hire her and then encourage her to get certified.

Diane Sheets, 42,
Jazzercise studio owner and area manager, Fremont, Ohio
Years in the business: 11

What drew you to Jazzercise?
I was a cheerleader in high school, and I loved exercise. My goal was to pursue a career in physical education when I graduated, but I married right away, had three kids and landed a quality-control job at a beer plant. Then when I was 32, I went to a Jazzercise demonstration and loved it. I knew when I started moving to that music that it was going to be something I wanted to do for a living.

So how did you get started?
The rule was that you had to be a Jazzercise student for six months before you could train to be a teacher. After six months you attended three workshops: The first was to determine whether the workshop trainers like the way you move. Fortunately, they did, and I was given the instruction needed to become a certified Jazzercise instructor. This included passing a test in exercise physiology, getting CPR

certified, memorizing 16 routines and being tested on two. After I became certified, I spent a few more days learning more about running a business. Once I did, I quit my job and started teaching ten classes a week.

Did you have other preparation for teaching exercise?
When I graduated high school I waitressed for a while, which helped me learn to relate to all kinds of people. It's a necessary skill to lead and motivate exercisers.

Where have you taught?
I began renting school gyms and taught at three different facilities a day. Then I moved all my classes to the YMCA for two years and had a great following there; I continued teaching ten classes a week. After a while I lost my time slot at the Y, but as luck would have it, my brother-in-law owned a building that used to be an auto body shop. We spent two months and $40,000 remodeling it, including putting in a wooden floor and air conditioning.

How are you set up now?
Our Jazzercise center offers 16 classes a week through spring and summer and a few more in winter. I teach ten of them. I have four franchised instructors who work on an hourly basis. Their pay is related to the number of students in their class, which is an incentive for them to attract new students.

What does being an area manager involve?
I'm a go-between for Jazzercise corporate headquarters and more than 30 franchised instructors in the Detroit area. I help new instructors promote themselves and set up their businesses; I also visit area Jazzercise centers regularly to make sure they are being run according to Jazzercise standards.

What do you like most about teaching Jazzercise?
I love the people and the friends I make in class. Making people feel good is fabulous! It's so rewarding to see success.

What do you like least about it?
I'm on the phone whenever I'm not teaching classes, and I'm usually in my office late. People have no idea of the work and preparation it takes to keep a business like this together.

Do you have to choreograph all the workouts?
No. With Jazzercise you get about 30 new routines every eight weeks, plus notes on exercise physiology and dance technique. You're never burnt out or bored. I think that's what keeps people coming back—the variety.

What achievements are you proudest of?
Jazzercize instructors were asked to be at the opening ceremonies for the anniversary of the Statue of Liberty: I got to teach at Giant Stadium. I did the same thing for the Special Olympics at Notre Dame. I performed on television, along with Whitney Houston, Barbara Mandrell and some other stars. There are opportunities for things you ordinarily wouldn't get to do. Plus, we hold charity fundraisers every year in our area, and that's always rewarding.

What does it take to be a successful Jazzercise instructor?
It takes leadership skills, drive and hard work to become successful. You have to be motivating and energetic. If you're having a crummy day, you can't let your students see it. If you want to own your own business, keep in mind that it's more work than you ever could imagine; you can find yourself thinking about and paying attention to nothing else but your business. You have to be willing to work hard, and you have to have a passion for it.

Dale Stine, 35, freelance group exercise instructor,
Molly Fox Studio and Equinox Fitness Club, New York, New York
Years in the business: ten

How did you first get involved in aerobics?
I was working on a cruise ship as a singer and dancer when I started taking an aerobics class given for the ship's employees. A year later I was in New York, walking down a street, when I ran into someone I knew through my music—I'm a trained opera singer. He convinced me to take aerobics at a fabulous studio called Jeff Martin's. After one

class Jeff invited me to take classes regularly and train to be an instructor.

What was teaching your first class like?
It was a surprise. I had been taking classes for five or six weeks when, one Sunday afternoon, Jeff told me to teach the next class. I said I wasn't ready: I hadn't really had much instruction yet; mostly I'd been working at the desk and being a monitor, which meant walking around the floor during class and correcting people on their form. But he wanted me to teach the class anyway, and before I knew it, I was doing ten a week.

Did you have to do things beyond teaching and monitoring?
I did a little of everything—signed people in for class, taught it and afterward made sure I'd collected all the money for the class. Then I'd clean up the studio and so forth.

What sort of preparation did you have for teaching?
I grew up with young parents who danced a lot, and I started taking dance in junior high and continued in college. So I knew how to move, which was the important thing at that time in aerobics. Then the more I taught, the more interested I became in why I was doing what I was doing. I began reading a lot about fitness and finally got certified.

So you felt you had a knack for teaching aerobics?
I think I had a natural sense of how the body should work and move. That was just as important to me after I acquired all the book knowledge. I believe either you're a good teacher or you're not. Some people just have more of a connection with groups of people.

What was the hardest thing about your work in the beginning?
There's a little bit of confusion at first because you have so many things going on at once—music blaring, counting the beats, cueing the class about the next step, keeping an eye on the person in the back row who looks like she's going to kill herself. Even now I experience that feeling when I teach in a new environment.

Do you find any of the aerobics routines harder to teach than others?
I find that much more concentration is required to teach step, because you have to break down each set of moves much more systematically for your students than with regular aerobic dance. It can be exhausting, but I remember the first couple of weeks I taught step; I came out with such a high.

How long did it take you to establish a reputation?
It took about four years to reach a point where studios were calling me and asking me to teach. But I started getting myself out there, networking, during my second year; I did a lot of charity work and meeting people, so my career just snowballed. These days there's a lot of opportunity to network because there are so many aerobics competitions, charity events, workshops, etc., where you can get your name out.

What are you doing now?
I teach classes at two different studios in Manhattan. I'm doing personal training, too—about 20 to 25 hours a week. I have eight clients, and most of them work out with me three times a week, either in their homes or at a gym. I see a lot of instructors going in this direction, mostly for financial reasons.

What do you like most about teaching?
I like that element of energy you feel in a room filled with people. That's why people take classes; they like that feeling, too.

What have you accomplished as an aerobics teacher that you're really proud of?
I'm chairperson for New York's City of Hope Workout for Hope. We had close to 600 people in New York come together to do aerobics and raise money for AIDS research.

What is one of the perks of being a group instructor?
I've done a lot of traveling related to my teaching, mostly in Switzerland and Sweden. But I've gone to Cyprus for two weeks also, with a group of teachers, and we spent two or three hours a day focusing on different types of classes like low impact or step, choreography—things like that.

Traveling is a great benefit; you get to see the world and meet people—and your expenses are paid.

What must a person do to get started as a group exercise teacher?

First, take different classes taught by different teachers. Make sure group teaching is something you really want to do, not just a way to make extra money. When you get up in front of a group of people, they expect something from you. It's important to get certified and stay abreast of developments in the industry. If you have any experience teaching at all, write up a resume. And be aggressive when you're job hunting: Ask for an interview with the manager of a club or a studio. They're always looking for new talent and will be willing to work with you if they see you're trying to learn. Talk to as many teachers as you can about your interest; it's really networking on a small scale.

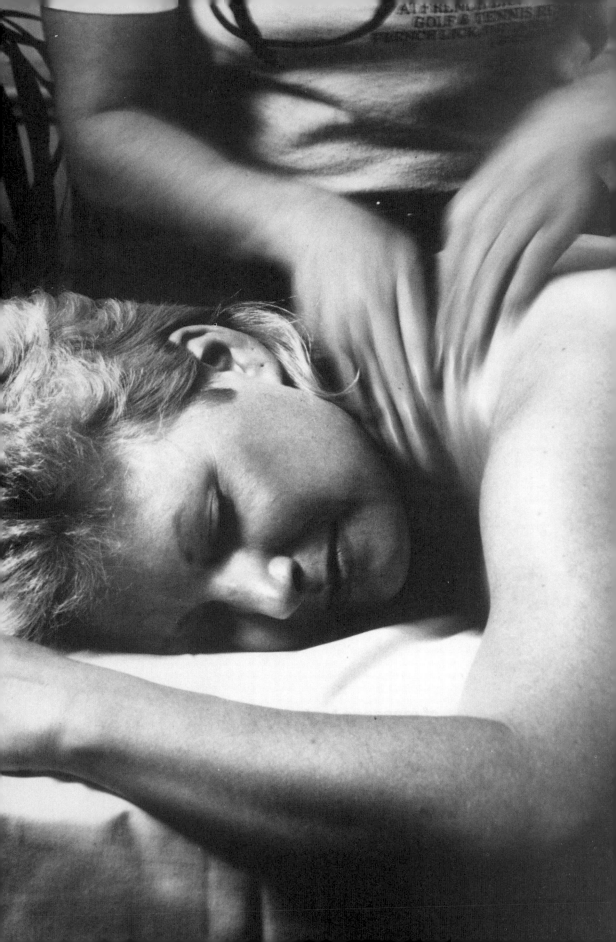

SPORTS MASSAGE THERAPIST

They're on call after professional ball games, amateur bike races and marathons— just about any time vigorous activity results in sore bodies and tight muscles. Sports massage therapists ease the stiff, aching bodies of athletes, and of amateur "weekend warriors." They are trained to find the source of muscular pain or injury by feel and then relieve the soreness and aid healing through a variety of massage techniques.

A thletes who believe in sports massage therapy say it can be a major factor in a gold-medal-winning performance. In fact, many European Olympic athletes wouldn't think of traveling without their therapist. But while sports massage is widely accepted in Europe, the practice is just beginning to gain popularity in the United States. Because sports massage has not yet attained full status as a "serious" profession, the field is wide open for highly skilled newcomers. And those newcomers are in demand, since there are relatively few sports massage therapists and a single therapist can handle only so many clients in a week.

Sports massage therapists usually are self-employed. They may work from an office or even a room in their home, or they may move around, bringing their services to health clubs, doctors' offices or other facilities that cater to the fitness minded. A smaller percentage of therapists work exclusively for sports teams or professional athletes, attending events and providing their services during training sessions.

Wherever sports massage therapists work, their day-to-day duties are basically the same: In sessions generally lasting an hour, they work on bare (partially sheet-covered) bodies, rubbing, rolling and pressing to work out tension and to stimulate blood flow to tender areas and prime muscles for action. To help their hands glide smoothly over skin, the therapists may use massage oil or lotion. For certain injuries they may apply a hot or cold pack.

As a sports massage therapist, you have to be sensitive to what clients are feeling as they are being rubbed and kneaded. It is physically demanding work, but if you enjoy dealing directly with people, if you have a desire to help heal, if you are interested in sports and those who play them, sports massage therapy could be just your ticket to a fulfilling fitness career.

What You Need to Know

❏ Anatomy (structure of the body, especially where the muscles are, where they are attached and how they move)

❏ Physiology (parts of the body and how they should work so you can recognize when a physical complaint needs medical attention)

❏ Basic first aid (especially if you will be working with a sports team or a competitive athlete at events)

❏ Simple business skills (how to schedule your time, budget and keep financial records, how to promote yourself, especially if you plan to be self-employed)

❏ Nutrition basics (enough to know whether a client's eating habits may be contributing to a lack of energy, for example)

Necessary Skills

❏ How to apply and combine massage strokes that work to relieve soreness or injury

❏ A "therapeutic touch" (ability to feel where muscles are tight and work on them with just enough pressure to relax them)

❏ Good body mechanics (moving safely and correctly as you work so that you don't injure yourself or your client)

❏ Attentiveness to clients' feelings (how to gauge the depth of a massage based on your client's response, whether through words or body language

Do You Have What It Takes?

❏ An interest or involvement in sports

❏ An enjoyment of hands-on work

❏ A desire to help heal

❏ An upbeat attitude (especially to provide a positive atmosphere for people who may be in pain)

Physical Attributes

❏ A healthy appearance
❏ Nonsmoker
❏ Good personal hygiene is critical as you will be in close physical contact with clients

Education

A high school diploma (or equivalent) is preferable for anyone attending massage school and necessary in states where a license is required.

Licenses Required

Only 15 states require therapists to be licensed. Therapists who live in other states can be voluntarily certified by the American Massage Therapy Association (AMTA). It offers a national certification exam twice a year. If you want to be a member of the AMTA Sports Massage Team, you must first get certified as a general massage therapist and do 28 hours of sports massage training (over the course of two weekends), work at seven different sporting events as both a pre-event and a post-event massage therapist and log ten hours of massage on two athletes in training.

Job Outlook

◆ **Competition for jobs:** favorable opportunities
Sports massage therapy is just taking off in this country. Evidence of its growing acceptance was heard during the 1991 Winter Olympics, when several big-name athletes frequently referred to massage during interviews. The field is wide open for qualified therapists.

The Ground Floor

◆ **Entry-level job:** therapist for a health club or massage clinic
Once you are trained, you can work as an independent therapist. But working as an employee will help you gain experience and hone your technique without the pressures that come with owning a business.

Private Practitioners

In addition to working on an average of 20 clients per week:

- ❑ Keep sheets and towels laundered and massage room neat
- ❑ Use hot- or cold-pack therapy on injuries when necessary
- ❑ Stay on top of financial affairs (keep track of bills, expenses, etc.)
- ❑ Advertise and promote business

Therapist for an Athlete or a Team

- ❑ Travel to sporting events
- ❑ Give energizing, muscle-loosening pre-event massages
- ❑ Work out post-event kinks and tightness
- ❑ Apply therapeutic massage to certain muscle injuries
- ❑ Sometimes provide basic first aid
- ❑ Sometimes be responsible for keeping water, sports drinks, snacks, towels and other items on hand during events
- ❑ Be available during practices to work on muscle problems unique to intense training

Therapists in private practice make their own hours, but most start their days between 10 A.M. and 12 P.M. and work until 7 or 8 P.M., because many people prefer a massage after their evening workout. Mondays are often busy, since amateur athletes who cram their exercise into the weekends come in to have overworked muscles unkinked. Some therapists are open on Saturdays. If you work for a health club, your hours will coincide with the times when most members use the facilities. If you work with athletes, you will be busiest after practice sessions and during events. Those hours will be set aside specifically for the team and the sport.

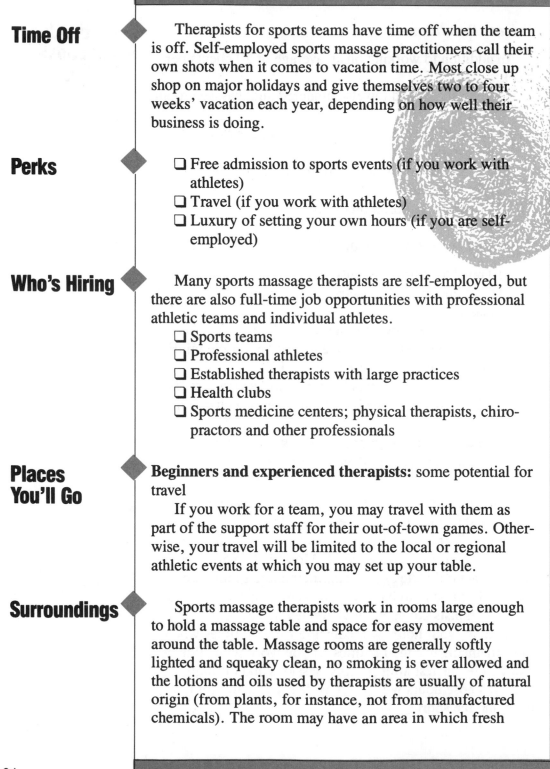

Time Off

Therapists for sports teams have time off when the team is off. Self-employed sports massage practitioners call their own shots when it comes to vacation time. Most close up shop on major holidays and give themselves two to four weeks' vacation each year, depending on how well their business is doing.

Perks

❑ Free admission to sports events (if you work with athletes)
❑ Travel (if you work with athletes)
❑ Luxury of setting your own hours (if you are self-employed)

Who's Hiring

Many sports massage therapists are self-employed, but there are also full-time job opportunities with professional athletic teams and individual athletes.
❑ Sports teams
❑ Professional athletes
❑ Established therapists with large practices
❑ Health clubs
❑ Sports medicine centers; physical therapists, chiropractors and other professionals

Places You'll Go

Beginners and experienced therapists: some potential for travel
If you work for a team, you may travel with them as part of the support staff for their out-of-town games. Otherwise, your travel will be limited to the local or regional athletic events at which you may set up your table.

Surroundings

Sports massage therapists work in rooms large enough to hold a massage table and space for easy movement around the table. Massage rooms are generally softly lighted and squeaky clean, no smoking is ever allowed and the lotions and oils used by therapists are usually of natural origin (from plants, for instance, not from manufactured chemicals). The room may have an area in which fresh

towels and sheets are kept, along with storage for oint-
ments, oils, vibrators and hot and cold packs. Often music
is piped in to help further relax clients.

The average fee for an hour's worth of sports massage
therapy is about $36. Practitioners may charge more in
major cities and a little less in small cities, towns and rural
areas. Therapists typically work on no more than 30 clients
a week. Multiply that number by $36, and you can see that
a motivated sports massage therapist can take in upward of
$50,000 a year. (There may, of course, be expenses, in-
cluding space rental.)
If you are an employee, expect to make less than the
average hourly fee.

◆ **Dollars
and Cents**

There is no official way to move up in the sports massage profession; the size of your business is the best indica-
tion of career advancement. If you are good, you will build
a steady, loyal clientele on whose business you can depend.
Sports team therapists may find that they can start with
local athletic clubs, gain a good reputation and move on to
professional teams.

◆ **Moving Up**

Wherever there are fitness addicts, there is potential
work for the sports massage therapist. While more people
in large cities may have the money to enjoy the benefits of
sports massage, it may be easier to launch your practice in
a small town where word-of-mouth advertising can send
more clients your way.

◆ **Where the
Jobs Are**

The American Massage Therapy Association is the
only group that sponsors continuing education courses and
certification in sports massage therapy.

◆ **Training**

It's estimated that at least 60 percent of massage therapists specializing in sports massage are women. This may
be because sports massage therapy has much of the same

◆ **The
Male/Female
Equation**

appeal as other professions that traditionally draw women: It requires a nurturing, sensitive personality and involves hands-on care.

Making Your Decision: What to Consider

The Bad News

❑ Stereotype of working in a "feel-good" job
❑ Building your own practice takes time
❑ Work itself is physically tiring
❑ Irregular work hours (for those who travel with athletes and teams)

The Good News

❑ Training is easy to get
❑ Relatively small initial investment is necessary to start a private practice
❑ Satisfaction of helping ease injury or pain
❑ Glamour of working with professional athletes (for team therapists)

Professional Organizations

American Massage Therapy Association
National Information Office
1130 West North Shore Avenue
Chicago, Illinois 60626
312-761-AMTA

Membership includes free subscriptions to massage publications, liability and life insurance (included in dues) as well as optional personal health insurance, access to legal advice, continuing education and certification programs and listing in a national registry of members.

WHAT IT'S
REALLY LIKE

John Kiegel, 30, sports massage therapist,
Vitality Works,
Albuquerque, New Mexico
Years in the business: three

How did you get interested in becoming a sports massage therapist?
Through bicycling. I used to do a lot of ultramarathons,
which is where I first saw sports massage in action. I was
working in a psychiatric hospital at the time and didn't feel
I was effective there. The benefits of sports massage
seemed more concrete and immediate: When you work on
someone, you can see a difference in an hour's time. I also
liked the lifestyle of the therapists.

What particularly did you like about their lifestyle?
Most therapists are their own bosses, so they have some
freedom to choose when and where they work. I liked the
idea of setting my own hours—and also of being able to
wear shorts and T-shirts to work, my kind of clothing. I
also liked the fact that sports massage therapists are healthy
people and often athletic.

How did you get started?

Because I was an athlete myself, I was receiving a lot of treatments. In fact, a massage therapy student had picked me to train on, so I got a massage every week for ten weeks. I asked many questions during those sessions and read books. Then I'd practice on family and friends. Finally I got interested enough to pick a school and get formal training.

What was your career plan?

I didn't really have a sports massage career targeted at that point. The massage school I attended emphasized other things as well as massage, but I've always been interested in working with athletes.

What was your first job like?

I got a job at a health club through a friend. I shared a room with two other male therapists and worked only on men because of the club's setup: The massage area was in the men's locker room. My clients paid me directly; I rented the room four nights a week. It was up to me to schedule my own appointments, supply my own linens and supplies and so forth. I stayed there for about nine months.

Is this a typical payment arrangement?

I believe that at most health clubs you are paid a percentage of what the club charges for the therapy, and the club provides the linens and the room and all that stuff.

Now where do you work on clients?

I rent a room at Vitality Works and share the costs for advertising, linens and supplies with six other therapists—three men and three women. But legally I'm my own businessman. I set my own hours, which is usually six days a week, with fewer hours on Saturdays. It comes to about 35 to 45 hours a week. I work mostly with injuries, and most of my appointments are in the late afternoon, between 3 and 6 P.M.

What was the hardest thing about getting started?

The business end of things—I had no idea what was involved in starting a business. It was hard to survive financially while getting set up because I had no idea how many expenses I would have (renting space, paying for electricity and the like) or how paying income taxes works for people who are self-employed. It took me a while to set up my bookkeeping so I could budget to cover all my bills.

What do you like most about being a sports massage therapist?

Seeing a change in people for the better. It could be an improvement in their health, their performance, a reduction in their injury rate, an increase in their bodies' flexibility. Most athletes come to me because they're broken and want to get fixed, so the injury is what we work on. It's nice to see them heal. Then we'll talk about their exercise routines—how they can get into better condition so they don't get hurt again. And as I've said, I also like the freedom to work when I want, although I do try to make myself available when customers need me. I do my workout in the morning and give clients sports massage therapy in the evening.

Is there anything about your job that you don't enjoy?

I didn't realize how risky it can be to have a small business; it isn't the most secure thing to do. I am very athletic myself, I bike, run, ski. If I were to crash and break something in my upper body, I'd be out of work.

What achievements are you most proud of?

I helped a serious runner who wanted to compete in a marathon but was having bad cramps. He worked with me for about three months before the race and set a personal record for himself. That was pretty neat.

Could you offer words of wisdom to anyone interested in becoming a sports massage therapist?

First, I'd encourage them to look into the business end of things. See what is involved in having your own business, because most massage therapists are self-employed. Make sure that appeals to you. Second, it helps to have good people skills because there's a lot of interaction between the therapist and the client. The work isn't just physical; you have to be able to talk to people easily and listen well.

Evonne Herkert, 36,
sports massage therapist
for the Cincinnati Bengals
and owner of The Right Touch,
Cincinnati, Ohio
Years in the business: seven

How did you get involved in sports massage therapy?
I was doing Swedish massage as a freelancer at a clinic
when the American Massage Therapy Association decided
to start a National Sports Massage Team. Doing massage
to make people feel good is rather basic, but I knew I
wanted to do something more, so I studied to become certified in sports massage therapy. I took the AMTA's test and
was one of only three people in Ohio who passed.

How did you end up with the Bengals?
Amazingly enough, one week after I found out I passed the
exam, Reggie Williams, one of the Bengals, walked into
the office looking to explore sports massage. It felt like
fate. I worked on him, and he really liked it. He gave my
name to Boomer Esiason, now the Bengals' quarterback.
Boomer was phenomenal about getting the others to try it.

Are the Bengals your only clients?
No. Working with the football players brought a lot of amateur athletes to my door. My practice now is really varied.
I work a lot with the amateurs to rehabilitate injuries. My
work helps football players keep in shape and injury free
by increasing their flexibility.

How is your practice set up?
I run my own office. It has two treatment rooms, a shower,
office and reception areas. Right now I have six therapists
working with me, and I opened another location in town. I
also have a sports massage team of 15 therapists from
around the state, and we specialize in giving massages to
athletes at cycling events.

**What inspired you to take your massage therapy in the
direction of sports?**
My grandfather was a pro boxer in the days when a boxer
was just a piece of meat. I have no memory of my grandfa-

ther ever being "right." After taking a constant beating as a boxer, the only thing he was mentally capable of was being a security guard at a factory. That was one of the things that made me want to help athletes so they don't get hurt.

What have your proudest accomplishments been?
I've had two: One, when the Bengals took me to the Super Bowl. I don't know of any other sports massage therapist who has been taken to the Super Bowl to work with the team. The last day the coach shook my hand, and that was a real glorious moment, since he had been doubtful about what my work could do.

The other accomplishment I'm proudest of has to do with Boomer Esiason. He suffered a groin injury and didn't think he was going to be able to play the next day. He came to me for treatment, and by the time he got off the table he had 20 percent more range of motion than when he got on—and he played the next day. In a press interview afterward he gave 80 percent of the credit for his being able to play to his massage therapist, and he mentioned my name.

What do you like most about working so closely with athletes?
The understanding it has given me about the incredible amount of drive these people have. I remember when the football players were on strike and I'd go to Boomer's house to give him a massage. He'd be on a conference call with 26 other team representatives, and he'd have me sit down and eat potato chips. I thought, how many people get to be on the inside of things like this?

Are you bothered when people ridicule massage?
You do run into animosity from trainers and doctors, although now trainers are starting to accept it more. I actually like the challenge of changing people's thinking around.

What's next for you?
There's a chance of my coming to work on the Bengals before every game. Right now I work on them mostly between games in my clinic. I don't believe any professional sports team has ever had a sports massage therapist work with them routinely.

How would you recommend someone get started in sports massage?

First, search out a school that has been AMTA approved and accredited to learn basic massage therapy. Through the AMTA you can get into conferences and workshops. There you can network, share ideas about running your business and find a tremendous source of support. If you want to work with pro athletes, find out who organizes sports tours, like golf tournaments, that come to the area and talk to them about your availability for those athletes. If you land some work, use it as a springboard to get your name out. And don't offer your services for free. People believe you get what you pay for, and if you don't charge, it cheapens what you're doing and makes it seem less important.

Cami Borodychuk, 24,
sports massage therapist and clinic owner, Moline, Illinois
Years in the business: three

How did you become interested in sports massage therapy?

I was working at a clinic with another therapist, doing basic Swedish massage, but I was getting bored with that. Then I discovered sports massage therapy when I heard about a big bike ride across the state of Iowa that several therapists go on. I decided to go through a training program for sports massage therapy. Now I work on athletes and have my own clinic.

How did you get started?

Whenever I heard of an event coming up I called to ask if the organizers wanted a sports massage therapist. If they did, I would go to the event with my table. Now I've moved up from doing it for free to charging for it. My next project is to work out an arrangement in which a local bike club pays me to give my services free to its cyclists.

How did you manage to obtain your own clinic?

First I worked out of a chiropractor's office. After a year I moved into an office space beside his, where I worked on clients I'd found myself and with patients he would send me. Finally I was financially stable enough to move into my present space: I went from a one-room office to a little building. At some point I might hire a therapist to work in an extra room I have, but right now I don't have any employees.

What are your hours like?
Mostly Monday through Friday, by appointment. The first appointment is usually at 10 A.M., the last between 5 and 6 P.M. On weekends I'll open for someone who can't get in during the week. There are a lot of Saturdays I don't work.

What is the hardest thing about getting established in this business?
Just getting your name out there, contacting the clubs. Sports massage isn't that well known; people say, "What's that?" particularly in smaller areas. One thing I recently did to promote myself was speak to a bike club about sports massage and its benefits. I took a table with me and gave a demonstration. I plan to contact some of the bigger organizations around here as well.

What do you like most about doing sports massage?
Being able to get outside when I do events. A lot of time I put my table under a shade tree. It's neat to have a line of people waiting to get on my table. Sports massage allows me to use my head a little and learn things. I always end up asking clients questions. For example, I've learned a lot about golf through sports massage; I could probably go out and play a pretty good game. But more to the point, the more people tell me about their sport, the more I understand it and the more I can help.

Do you play sports yourself?
Sports massage has gotten me into activity, rather than the other way around. When you're working on people who are in good shape, you find you want to be in good shape yourself.

What do you like least about your job?
This is minor, but I can get really dirty because a lot of the people who crawl onto my table are still sweating and my hands wind up sticky and grimy. I don't like it when someone goes into a cramp on me either; it puts me on edge for a little while. When you have a bunch of people standing

around and someone starts to scream and hold on to a body part, it doesn't look good. But I do like it when I can get rid of the cramp. I also have to face a lot of ignorance from people who don't understand sports massage. Sometimes I'll work on somebody, and then their buddies will give them a hard time about it—they don't know enough about massage themselves.

Does that kind of reaction make it hard to keep going?
Not really. Sports massage therapy is a rewarding thing. You learn about all sorts of injuries and how to treat them. Once I worked with a guy who did a seven-mile run without drinking anything. He was suffering from hyperthermia; he got overheated. I was able to recognize this and tell him what to do.

What advice would you give to someone interested in a career in sports massage?
First, go through a good sports massage training course. Then start out by calling sports clubs in your area; offer to speak about massage and give demonstrations. When I started out I didn't charge anything, but now I do. People respect you if you're getting paid.

What would you like to do next?
Besides working with baseball and basketball teams, I'm thinking about trying to become sports massage chairperson for Illinois. That job would let me coordinate a lot of events and teach sports massage therapy. It would also give me a chance to educate the public about sports massage. I think it would be wonderful for people to see that not all massages are in dimly lit rooms with scented oils.

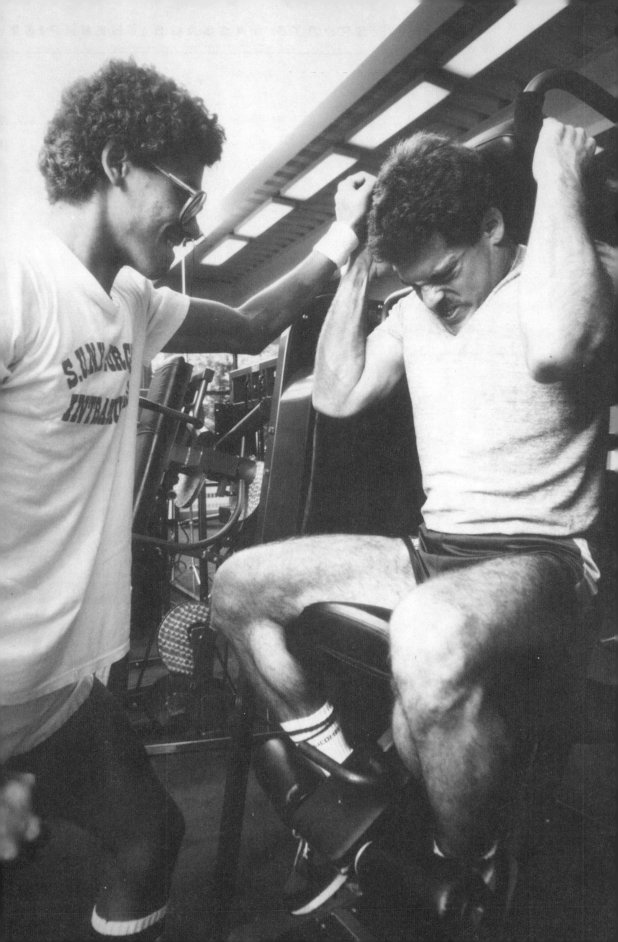

Personal trainers are no longer only for the fit and famous. These days ordinary people serious about getting in good shape are budgeting their time and money to hire one. They know that a fitness professional who "works out" clients on a one-to-one basis can give them something another instructor can't: personalized motivation and a fitness routine that focuses on their own physical strengths, weaknesses and goals.

If you choose to become a personal trainer, you must know the human body—how it is put together, how it moves, how it responds to exercise, what its limitations are. You must be well schooled in the principles of exercise training and be able to put together a fitness regimen (including aerobic conditioning, strength training and stretching) that gets good results.

37

Trainers can recognize when a routine is not working and can spot an injury that needs special attention.

Because you may work with several different personalities in a single day, your own personality must sometimes change to adjust to the mood of each client. The trainer has to be able to cope with cranky people, let criticism roll off his or her back and even be prepared to hear details about a client's private life.

Most trainers begin as employees of health clubs or studios that specialize in one-on-one workouts, or as assistants to established trainers. This helps them gain both the experience and the clientele to strike out on their own. They can then start up their own training facility or become traveling trainers, going to people's homes or from club to club. A talented few even work exclusively with celebrities, which can be glamorous as well as grueling, since the trainer may be expected to be available at the drop of a hat or the signing of a movie contract.

But whether a trainer's clientele consists of the year's hottest stars or ordinary people, his or her profession can be one of the most fulfilling and high paying in the fitness business. Indeed, the financial rewards can enhance the satisfaction personal trainers get from motivating and helping others to make health and fitness a way of life.

What You Need to Know

- ❑ Anatomy (where bones, muscles and joints are located and how they work together)
- ❑ Kinesiology (how the body moves)
- ❑ Exercise physiology (how activity affects the body)
- ❑ How to determine what kind of physical condition a person is in
- ❑ Principles of exercise training (how to achieve aerobic fitness, muscle strength and flexibility with exercise)
- ❑ Basic nutrition (how foods affect weight loss and gain, which foods deliver energy, basic good eating habits)
- ❑ Sports medicine basics (enough to recognize minor injury and be able to recommend the proper specialist for treatment)

Necessary Skills

- ❑ Ability to spot a client who is lifting weights (make sure moves are performed correctly and safely and, when necessary, assist with lifting a weight)
- ❑ Motivational know-how (to keep even the most discouraged exerciser on track)
- ❑ Problem solving (being able to find new approaches to exercise training when others aren't working or to put together a complete exercise program with little or no equipment)
- ❑ Leadership (the ability to take charge of exercise sessions firmly without seeming bossy)
- ❑ Communication (listening to clients without making them feel you are judging them; providing information, instruction and responses clearly and briefly; establishing comfortable eye contact)

Do You Have What It Takes?

- ❑ A personal interest in exercise and in staying healthy and fit

◆ **Getting into the Field**

❑ A desire to help others benefit from exercise and improve their image—physically and mentally

❑ Patience

❑ An easygoing attitude about sudden changes of schedule (when clients want to cancel or delay regular workouts at the last minute)

❑ A desire for career independence (should you decide to become self-employed as a freelancer)

❑ A thick skin (not getting bent out of shape when a client complains or criticizes your advice)

❑ Stamina (you will often be working out alongside clients)

Physical Attributes

❑ Strong, fit-looking physique (you will want to be an example of the positive effects of exercise)

❑ Nonsmoker

❑ Good personal hygiene is a must, as you will be in close physical contact with clients

Education

A high school diploma is preferred. An associate degree in a fitness field is a plus. Since people who work out with trainers often know quite a lot about exercise, nutrition and other areas of health, they expect trainers to be equally informed.

Licenses Required

No licensing is required, but personal trainers should be certified by a professional organization such as the American Council on Exercise (ACE) or the Aerobics and Fitness Association of America (AFAA). CPR (cardiopulmonary resuscitation, a set of skills used when someone has stopped breathing or his or her heart has stopped) is generally required of those who start out working in health clubs or as assistants to established trainers.

Competition for jobs: increasingly competitive

The personal training industry is on the upswing since more and more people are recognizing the value of fitness routines designed specially for their personal needs. They are using such training as their sole exercise activity or as part of their total exercise program. The more education a trainer has, the better he or she will do as job competition grows. However, even though some employers expect trainers to have four years or more of college education in a fitness field, others respect the well-rounded knowledge nondegree trainers gain through the certification process, and they will hire such applicants if their personal qualities and experience also fill the bill.

◆ **Job Outlook**

Entry-level job: trainer in a health club or as an assistant to an established trainer

If you hope to eventually go into business for yourself, working as an assistant to a seasoned trainer will give you the business sense you need to be self-employed.

◆ **The Ground Floor**

Beginners (usually work at a health club or assist an established freelance trainer)

◆ **On-the-Job Responsibilities**

❑ Design fully developed fitness routines for individuals based on their goals and current fitness levels (a trainer may administer health questionnaires to new exercisers; generally the health of a client is determined through testing done by a physiologist)
❑ Work one-on-one with a client, setting and adjusting exercise machinery, spotting weightlifting moves, demonstrating exercises, often participating in the workout
❑ Update exercise routines
❑ Do paperwork, such as follow-up evaluations of clients' progress

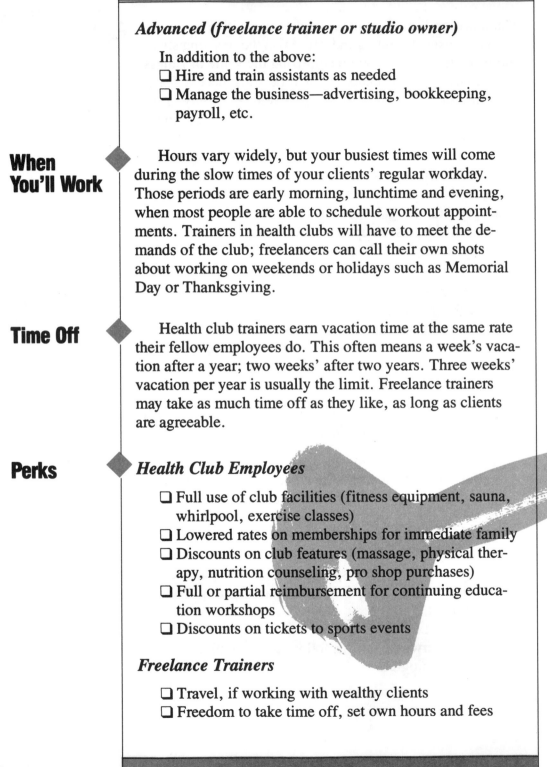

Advanced (freelance trainer or studio owner)

In addition to the above:
- ❏ Hire and train assistants as needed
- ❏ Manage the business—advertising, bookkeeping, payroll, etc.

When You'll Work

Hours vary widely, but your busiest times will come during the slow times of your clients' regular workday. Those periods are early morning, lunchtime and evening, when most people are able to schedule workout appointments. Trainers in health clubs will have to meet the demands of the club; freelancers can call their own shots about working on weekends or holidays such as Memorial Day or Thanksgiving.

Time Off

Health club trainers earn vacation time at the same rate their fellow employees do. This often means a week's vacation after a year; two weeks' after two years. Three weeks' vacation per year is usually the limit. Freelance trainers may take as much time off as they like, as long as clients are agreeable.

Perks

Health Club Employees

- ❏ Full use of club facilities (fitness equipment, sauna, whirlpool, exercise classes)
- ❏ Lowered rates on memberships for immediate family
- ❏ Discounts on club features (massage, physical therapy, nutrition counseling, pro shop purchases)
- ❏ Full or partial reimbursement for continuing education workshops
- ❏ Discounts on tickets to sports events

Freelance Trainers

- ❏ Travel, if working with wealthy clients
- ❏ Freedom to take time off, set own hours and fees

❑ Personal training studios
❑ Established freelance trainers
❑ Health clubs
❑ YMCAs, parks and recreation facilities and other
community centers
❑ Hotels
❑ Resorts
❑ Cruise ships

◆ Who's Hiring

Beginners: little travel potential
Experienced trainers: some travel potential

◆ Places You'll Go

If you train wealthy clients who like to keep fit when they are on the road, you may travel frequently, often flying first class and staying in luxury hotels or at the family ski lodge or beach house. Personal trainers who establish themselves as tops in the field may also be invited to teach workshops and lecture in other cities.

The personal trainer's workspace may be in a health club, Y or other fitness center, with plenty of machinery available—and other exercisers to work around. Depending on the time of day, noise levels may be high.

◆ Surroundings

Trainers who travel to the homes of their clients will make do with whatever space is available—a family room with furniture pushed aside, an empty basement or garage, a large patio. Wealthy clients may have a special room for exercise, complete with some equipment. Otherwise trainers may bring along a few items for the workout.

Set-ups in studios that specialize in personal training will vary from plain and simple to sleek and luxurious.

What you make as a personal trainer depends on where you work and how much experience you have. If you are a beginner and employed by a health club or other fitness facility, you will get a cut (40 to 60 percent) of what the client pays the club for your services. The same goes for assistants to established trainers. You may make considera-

Dollars and Cents

bly more money when you strike out on your own: To date, the going hourly rates for one-on-one training sessions range from as little as $7 in suburban towns to hundreds of dollars in cities like New York and Los Angeles. The average fee per hour is $25. Trainers should check out the prices of similar services in their area to avoid charging too much or too little. Freelancers who go to clients' homes may eventually add on about 25 percent to their hourly rate to cover travel costs.

Moving Up

The key to moving up from health club employee or assistant to a self-employed trainer is performance. If you are doing your job well, helping clients see results and being one of the most requested trainers where you work, you should have little trouble breaking away to start your own business. It is also important to keep up with current training trends by reading journals and attending workshops, taking continuing education courses and renewing your certification.

Where the Jobs Are

Fitness centers, YMCAs and the like are found throughout the United States and can provide a place of employment for the trainer just starting out. Facilities that specialize in personal training may be harder to find outside major metropolitan areas (New York, Los Angeles, Chicago, Atlanta, etc.). However, with more people interested in personal training, the freelancer can drum up a steady clientele just about anywhere, except perhaps in very rural areas.

Training

Personal trainers have their pick from a number of certification programs. Among the most widely recognized professional groups that offer certification are ACE, AFAA and the Cooper Institute for Aerobics Research.

The Male/Female Equation

Personal training has been a male-dominated field. But as the profession has evolved, more women than men are participating in workshops and applying for certification.

The Bad News

❏ Moving up from health club employee to personal trainer may take a while
❏ Beginning salaries low
❏ Work day starts early, ends late
❏ Celebrity trainers are usually at the beck and call of employers

The Good News

❏ Working for an established employer can help beginners build a strong clientele
❏ Possibility of making a good living over time
❏ Setting one's own hours (self-employed trainers)
❏ Opportunity to keep in top physical shape while you work out with clients

◆ **Making Your Decision: What to Consider**

Going Solo: The Art of Personal Training
by Douglas Brooks, M.S.
How to find clients, develop workouts and keep exercisers motivated, as well as tips on setting up shop as a trainer. (Available from Moves International, 1849 Sawtelle Blvd., Suite 101, Los Angeles, California 90025; 213-312-5055; $24.95 plus shipping and handling.)

The Personal Trainer Success Manual
by D.S. Ching
Covers everything from training techniques to business strategies. (Available from The Personal Trainer, Inc., P.O. Box 15242, Honolulu, Hawaii 96830; $59.95 plus shipping and handling.)

◆ **Recommended Reading**

WHAT IT'S REALLY LIKE

Susan Pauly, 40,
self-employed personal trainer,
Los Angeles, California
Years in the business: 15 (four as a
personal trainer)

How did you get started as a personal trainer?
I eased into it. I was an aerobics manager for a health club
chain in Los Angeles, where I both trained other instructors
and taught classes. People started asking me to help them
individually at home. So for a while I just dabbled in personal training. I've been doing it full time for about four
years.

**What made you decide to switch from aerobics instruc-
tor to personal trainer?**
I liked the idea of being my own boss and I really enjoyed
working one-on-one with people.

How did you get your business underway?
When I decided to strike out on my own, the first thing I
did was get my ACE certification in personal training. In a

way I had a head start because as an aerobics manager I knew more about fitness than the average exercise instructor.

Where did your first clients come from?
A few trainers I knew didn't have time to work with some of their clients, so they asked if I could take on the overflow. Then that first year a trainer left town and sold me her client list.

Is this a typical way to start a business in personal training?
Yes and no. Word of mouth is it. The best way to get clients, I think, is to take on other trainers' extras or through referrals by your own clientele. But you usually don't pick up ten clients overnight by buying someone else's business. A friend of mine who has been a personal trainer for many years told me that any time you take on someone else's client list, about half of them are going to leave. But they all stayed with me for a long time, and that was a real boost to my confidence.

Describe what you do on the job.
I go to people's homes; occasionally I use a gym. I see most of my clients twice a week, sometimes three times. Sessions are about an hour long. Many of the people I work with have a very low level of fitness and don't need a lot of equipment. We walk, stretch, do floor work. The clients who exercise usually already have enough of the things we need for strength training, like a bench and free weights. If we do cardiovascular work outdoors—running, cycling, walking—I go along, too.

What was hardest thing about being a trainer during the first few years?
Getting over feeling nervous about meeting someone new and figuring out what I could do for them and what they wanted from me. You're walking into the home of someone you've never met before and saying, "Here I am and I'm going to charge you all this money." That's scary; everyone has their own agenda and you want them to be successful. It's a lot of pressure. It took me about a year to get past that.

What do you enjoy most about being a trainer?
There's a lot of immediate gratification, like when you finish a session and your client says "I feel great," or when someone's body starts to change for the better. Plus I can schedule my time any way I want within reason. Personal training also is a constant challenge, and I enjoy that. Clients will ask you anything and you have to have an answer. If you don't, you have to find it. I'm taking classes at the University of California, Los Angeles, in exercise physiology, strength training, anatomy, biomechanics and nutrition to keep up with things.

Is there anything you don't like about your work?
I'd like to have more clients. It can get a little iffy sometimes when a few drop out.

What are you most proud of?
Hopefully all my clients have achieved something by working with me. I have one woman who lost 30 pounds. I have two women who have stayed motivated for two years; they're right in there working out regularly, eating right and doing really well.

Can you offer some advice to someone who aspires to be a personal trainer?
There are a lot of trainers out there who don't know what they're doing. You may fake your way through for a while, but clients are going to start asking questions, so you have to get as much education as you can. A club situation is a good way to start, to get experience with the equipment and to learn how to design workouts and train people. You have to be careful about breaking rules when you're ready to go out on your own: Don't hand out your card on club property or try to "steal" clients from other trainers.

Doug Dearth, 26,
assistant personal trainer,
Los Angeles, California
Years in the business: one

How did you break into the field?
I got into body building and competing as a hobby while I
was the manager of a restaurant. Eventually customers and
employees who knew about my training began approaching
me for tips on diet and training, and I started working with
two people on a part-time basis. Then another employee at
the restaurant, the wife of an established trainer, Tony Cortes, introduced me to Tony. He has a lot of celebrity clients
who he gets in shape for movie roles and so forth; he en-
couraged me to quit the restaurant business and work for
him. I was unsure at first because I was making decent
money. But I've always been a person who makes things
happen, so I decided to take the plunge. One thing that
really motivated me to become a trainer was that I saw a lot
of people making a living training clients incorrectly, taking
advantage of their lack of knowledge.

What were the first steps?
Tony required that I get certified, which I did through the
Aerobics and Fitness Association of America. The AFAA
offered a three-day weekend of workshops and training
before the exam. I also did an internship with Tony: I went
on appointments with him to learn his way of doing things.
He tested me by having me write up the programs I would
design for hypothetical clients based on their body fat percentage, goals, fitness level and the like. When I met my
first client, Tony came along for the consultation and
helped me write up the initial program; he also came to the
first workout I did with a client.

Is this a good way to start out?
Working with a successful trainer is an excellent way to
start out. If I had had to start all on my own, I would have
had a lot of trouble financially because I didn't understand
all the in's and out's of the business. Tony showed me a lot
of shortcuts that saved me from making mistakes.

After the internship, were you on your own?
Yes. Even though I'm technically considered Tony's assistant, I have my own clients. Many are those Tony does not
have time to work with. I didn't do any advertising except
for putting some business cards in a few sporting goods
stores.

**What was the most difficult thing you had to deal with
in the beginning?**
Learning to be patient and understanding with people who
have been overweight all their lives and just can't seem to
get motivated. They don't want to work out but know they
should. Since exercise had always been a part of everyday
life for me, I had trouble understanding why someone was
paying me to show them how to do something and then not
doing it. It was easy to get frustrated.

How did you overcome clients' lack of motivation?
I tried to make the workouts fun because if you don't enjoy
exercise, you aren't going stick with it. I also encourage
my clients to make fitness a lifetime commitment.

What is your work like now?
I train about half my clients in their homes and the other
half in local gyms. I don't carry around much equipment,
just a minitrampoline or maybe a platform for step ups. I
also have some training in nutrition analysis, so I work up
diets for my clients and for many of Tony's.

What do you enjoy most about your job?
I like helping people feel positive about themselves. I know
how good it feels to have someone admire the way I look
or the discipline I have. I enjoy hearing my clients say
they've had to buy smaller clothes or have gotten a
compliment.

What do you like least?
For one thing, the hours. Here in L.A. people want to exercise before work or after. I get up at 4:00 A.M. so I can
train my first clients by 5 or 5:30. There's a lot of driving
around and juggling schedules, too, and that can be a pain.
You can't schedule yourself too closely because people
always run a little late. In fact, organization is probably the
key to my getting it all going. Also, sometimes I don't feel

like being upbeat, but I have to be: You have to be motivating every day, whether you feel like it or not.

What achievements are you most proud of?
One, I've helped a couple of trainers get started the same way Tony helped me. Personal training is competitive, but there's still a lot of business out there, and I'm happy to share what I know with newcomers. Two, I have a client, a guy, who just turned 40. He wasn't athletic in school, and this was the first time he'd really exercised. I had been working with him for about four months when he came to me with an application to run a five-kilometer race. His attitude was, he was going to run it, walk it, crawl it, whatever it would take to finish. Because of our training together, he's doing something at 40 he wouldn't have thought of doing at 21.

Can you offer any advice to someone who wants to get into personal training?
Visit a physical therapy center, college sports training center or health club to see what a trainer does. Read everything you can about training, anatomy, physiology, nutrition. Work out yourself, so you know what it feels like to exercise and so you'll be in good shape. Above all, get certified: It's important proof that you're a professional, that you know what you're doing and that you're worth the higher rate you may decide to charge.

Patty Smith, 33,
personal trainer,
Garland, Texas
Years in the business: less than one

How did you get started as a personal trainer?
Weekdays I was in the corporate world working with computers; evenings I taught aerobics part time at three different places. I began realizing that people often had poor exercise techniques and that I had the knowledge to help them. Students with questions seemed to really appreciate the assistance I gave them, and that gave me a lot of personal satisfaction. At the same time, I was very unhappy

with my computer job and realized I should change fields completely.

Did you just jump right in then?

No, there was too much financial security at the corporation. So, I used my weekends and even some vacation time to attend conferences and workshops to further my education about fitness. However, when there was a major layoff at my company I lost my job, and I used that opportunity to break into fitness full time. I went to the Cooper Institute for Aerobics Research in Dallas to get my personal trainer certification.

What did that involve?

Certification there takes a week. You go to classes from eight to five every day and have homework. At the end you have a practicum as well as a written test to get your certification. It's very intense but very good.

Besides teaching aerobics and certification, what preparation did you have for personal training?

I've always been active. I've done a lot of running, walking and biking, and in high school I was on a dance squad that performed during half-time at football and basketball games.

How have you drummed up business in the few months you've been certified?

Currently I have three clients who I got through teaching aerobics. I'm having business cards made up, as well as a brochure that explains my rates and what I can offer as a trainer. The competition is tough—you go to a health club and they already have ten trainers. So you have to keep getting out and networking; you have to let people know you're in business and that you have a lot of knowledge.

Do you train your clients at health clubs?

Right now I do. The club I use allows personal trainers to work there if they are certified and have liability insurance. Though some clubs take a cut of a trainer's fee, I don't have to pay one there; this club figures I may bring in potential new members.

What do you enjoy most about being a trainer?

The contact I have with people and helping them improve

their health. For me it's a win-win situation: I get personal satisfaction from helping people, and they get the benefits of improved fitness. I also feel I am controlling my own destiny. For the most part I can say, "Yes," or "No," to appointments and set up my schedule based on my own needs. Mostly I work mornings and evenings. The down side is that sometimes I have very late nights followed by very early mornings. But I'm an active person and have a million things going on; the hours I work let me fit the other things in.

What do you like least about the job?
It's very competitive, and that's hard for me. You have to be a salesperson to win clients. I figure eventually I'll find the key words that will get people to buy my services. I have to pay for my own medical benefits and vacations, too, but that's true for anyone who works for herself.

What are your goals as a personal trainer?
I want to keep my hand in aerobics but do personal training 60 to 70 percent of the time. I would love to train clients in their homes, using their equipment and facilities so they don't feel they have to join a club to get a good workout. A lot of people around here have pools they don't use, for example. I'd like to start up small group exercise sessions at their houses so staying fit would also become a social event. In such a situation people would stay with it because it's fun.

Can you offer any suggestions to personal trainers who are just starting out?
Don't do anything until you are certified. Once you've done that, start networking. Some say networking is not as important as it's claimed to be. But in this field you have to get out there and meet people, get your name out to people who can help your business expand in the community. I try to network with other personal trainers.

If you have ever used a health club, you have seen them in action: handing out towels, scheduling lesson times and conducting tours of the exercise rooms and classes. A health club's sales and service staff are its welcomers and problem solvers. Their hospitality and helpfulness—or lack of it—are more important than the equipment and look of the facility.

How effectively a club's sales and service staff performs is vitally important to its success. If a potential client's first encounter with the front desk receptionist is pleasant and informative, for example, the chances that the visitor will sign up usually increase. If the meeting is unpleasant, the club will seem unattractive, even if it does offer the newest equipment and fancy locker rooms.

55

As a member of the sales and service staff, you might greet clients at the front desk, field questions and complaints, sell memberships, give tours of the club to prospective members, make sure locker rooms are in order—or a combination of several of these duties.

Salespeople (also called membership representatives) have the special responsibility of showing off the club and all it has to offer. A natural talent for selling, a friendly personality, a commitment to fitness and some knowledge about exercise are musts. Looking fit and healthy is important, too, because a salesperson is visible proof that what the club has to offer works.

Some sales and service staff move up to become assistant managers or managers of the club; others gain the responsibility of overseeing the entire sales staff. For the fitness buff who wants a no-sweat job in this industry, the business side may be just right.

What You Need to Know

❑ What fitness is all about and what sort of results are realistic for a new exerciser

❑ New developments in the fitness industry (so you will be able to give potential clients an idea of how your club measures up to others)

Necessary Skills

❑ Ability to use a variety of office equipment—cash registers, fax machines, computers, telephone systems, credit card processing machines, copiers

❑ Basic math (from making change in the pro shop to calculating complicated payment terms for new members)

❑ A thorough understanding of the terms of a membership contract

❑ Salesmanship (how to present a product and sell it)

❑ Good phone manners

Do You Have What It Takes?

❑ A true personal interest in health and fitness

❑ A friendly, pleasant personality

❑ A love of meeting new people

❑ The courage to make calls to strangers or make follow-up sales calls (checking back with people who have requested information about the club or who have taken a tour)

❑ Diplomacy (especially to resolve problems without offending club members who have complaints)

Physical Attributes

❑ Physically fit, well-groomed appearance

❑ Nonsmoker

Education

A high school diploma is necessary.

◆ **Getting into the Field**

Licenses Required

Some clubs require all personnel to be certified in cardiopulmonary resuscitation (CPR, a set of skills used when someone has stopped breathing or his or her heart has stopped).

Job Outlook

Competition for jobs: favorable opportunities

Like other jobs in the fitness industry, openings in sales and service mirror the continuing growth of fitness centers and clubs.

The Ground Floor

Entry-level job: receptionist or sales representative

Both jobs are good starting points and can help you learn the health club business.

On-the-Job Responsibilities

Beginners (receptionists)

❑ Meet and greet new and potential clients
❑ Sign in members
❑ Help members in a variety of ways, from doling out towels to calling a cab
❑ Answer questions (either in person or over the phone) regarding club hours, class schedules, membership fees, the facility's location and nearby public transportation, etc.
❑ Put members in touch with other staffers (for instance, referring a member with a diet question to the club nutritionist)
❑ Keep locker rooms clean and well stocked with towels, soap, shampoo (at some clubs)
❑ Give tours of the club

Experienced

❑ Open or close the club (which may mean working with complicated security systems or handling cash)
❑ Fill in for an assistant manager when that person is not in

Beginners (sales representative)

- ❑ Show prospective members around the club (if this is not the responsibility of the front desk person)
- ❑ Answer all questions about equipment, classes, education of trainers, prices of club features, such as massage and physical therapy
- ❑ Know the facts and figures about membership contracts and fees and be able to present this information clearly
- ❑ Close sales (handle contracts, payments and other paperwork)
- ❑ Make follow-up calls

Advanced (sales manager)

- ❑ Oversee sales staff
- ❑ Hire and train new membership representatives
- ❑ Help develop literature or events promoting the club

◆ When You'll Work

Because most health clubs are open longer than eight hours (16 hours is more typical), receptionists work eight-hour shifts that may begin as early as 6 or 7 A.M. or not begin until early afternoon. Sales reps usually work when potential customers are most likely to drop in; during lunch hour and after work are prime times.

◆ Time Off

Full-time health club staff get full-time benefits. Generally, this means that after a year of employment you will earn a week of vacation; after two years you will earn two weeks. Three weeks' vacation is usually the limit. You may be expected to work on holidays.

◆ Perks

- ❑ Use of club facilities (fitness equipment, sauna, whirlpool, classes, etc.)
- ❑ Lowered rates on memberships for immediate family
- ❑ Discounts on club features (massage, physical therapy, nutrition counseling, pro shop purchases)
- ❑ Discounts on tickets to professional sports events (offered by some clubs)

Who's Hiring

❏ Health clubs
❏ Hotels and spas with fitness centers

Places You'll Go

Beginners: no travel
Experienced sales reps: occasional local travel
Reps who pitch to corporate clients sometimes make presentations and visit the offices of prospective members.

Surroundings

If you work as a receptionist, you will probably be stationed behind a large desk or counter, surrounded by office equipment. During the club's busiest hours you may be caught up in a flurry of activity as members rush in to make their favorite class or to get an early start on their workouts. Salespeople are usually all over the club, showing it off to potential members. Signing up new members may take place in a private office or a cubbyhole, depending on the size of the club.

Dollars and Cents

Receptionists may make from minimum wage to $7 or $8 an hour with a potential for overtime (at a rate of time-and-a-half). Sometimes earnings are based only on commissions from sales; sometimes earnings include a small hourly wage plus commission. The most successful sellers may also increase their paychecks with bonuses.

Moving Up

Promotions are usually based on performance. The salesperson who consistently signs up new members may very likely move up to sales manager. Front desk personnel who are always pleasant and helpful to members, who keep up with changes in the club and in the fitness industry in general and who make no mistakes handling money have an excellent chance of taking on more responsibilities—and eventually landing a managerial position.

Where the Jobs Are

Large cities and surrounding suburbs boast the most health clubs. However, fitness facilities can also be found in all but the most rural of settings.

Health club sales and service personnel are usually trained by more senior sales and service people in the club. Employees who want to stay current on fitness trends can keep themselves well informed about new equipment, classes and viewpoints about exercise and health by reading magazines.

◆ **Training**

Both men and women can, and do, excel as health club employees. The ratio of men to women is about 50-50.

◆ **The Male/Female Equation**

◆ **Making Your Decision: What to Consider**

The Bad News

❑ Minimum-wage pay for service
❑ Dealing with difficult club members
❑ Routine locker room duties
❑ Salespeople may earn only a commission, not a salary

The Good News

❑ Plenty of perks, including full use of club facilities
❑ Potential for meeting people and making new friends
❑ As you prove yourself, increased opportunities to take charge and make decisions affecting clients
❑ Big bonuses possible when sales are high (salespeople)

WHAT IT'S REALLY LIKE

Mary Ann Hynes, 24,
sales representative and
reception desk manager,
Club Fit, Jefferson Valley, New York
Years in the business: one and a half

How did you get your job as a sales rep?
I answered an ad in the newspaper. I was already a member
of Club Fit and enjoyed the sporty atmosphere a lot. So I
applied and was hired.

What did the job involve?
I started out working at the front desk as a receptionist and
as a salesperson. I spent 20 hours at the desk and 20 hours
selling. Within six months I was promoted to training coordinator. I worked with new employees at the desk and designed training programs for them.

What do you do now as a desk manager?
I oversee the staff receptionists, who handle court reserva-
tions and registration for lessons and lectures, sign in members when they come to work out and answer the phones. I
make sure everything runs smoothly and that the money
taken in that day matches up with what the intake should

be. On some days I serve as manager on duty, which means I handle any complaints and take care of anything that goes wrong.

Do you still handle sales?
I spend half of my time selling memberships. I give tours of the club to potential clients, provide information about the club's features and make follow-up phone calls to people who have toured the club. I write letters to people who came in and didn't join, trying to motivate them to take a look at the club again. I handle the actual paperwork for sales, too.

What sort of preparation did you have for your job at the club?
I did a lot of intramural sports in school, and I've always worked out myself. That's helped because it meant I understood exercise machines and training techniques. This all gave me a fitness state of mind, but that's about all the preparation I had before I came on board. Once I was hired, though, I did a month-long training session in which I learned about the club, our rates, sales techniques and the like.

What was hardest thing about being new on the job?
There were so many things to learn. In just four weeks I had to learn everything at the front desk plus all the aspects of selling, contracts and club rules. Getting all this straight was tough: You're dealing with different people all the time, so rules have to be changed constantly. You have to know how far you can bend the rules.

What do you like most about what you're doing?
I like the constant contact with people. I really enjoy helping people solve problems and seeing new people progress in their workouts and feel better about themselves. I've always wanted a job in which I didn't have to sit behind a desk all the time.

What do you like least?
Probably the paperwork. We have a lot of bill collecting, for instance, and I just don't enjoy that. It involves phone calls that you don't really want to make to clients about late payments.

Have you accomplished anything you're especially proud of in the year and a half you've worked at the club?

Just moving up into a management position so quickly. You usually have to be here a number of years to be considered for that position. I've been the top seller for the past five months.

What advice do you have for anyone interested in working in health club sales?

Start networking, sending your resume out to let people see you. Try to get a job at a club in the summer, working in the fitness center if you're certified, working the desk or in the nursery or cafe—anything to get a foot in the door, because a lot of clubs hire from within. Then, if you're good, people will notice it. Visit different clubs and try to meet the membership director or club manager. Get in shape yourself. That's a big plus because if you're selling the club, you need to be fit, too. Members like to see that you use the club you represent.

Kelly Heffron, 26, sales representative, The Fitness Center at The Cooper Institute for Aerobics Research, Dallas, Texas
Years in the business: one and a half

What do you do as a sales representative?

I work in membership sales, but one of my main goals is to pull in corporate accounts, companies who want to start an aerobics program for their employees. There are different kinds of corporate memberships. Some companies will pay complete membership fees for all their employees; some will pay a percentage of their employees' membership fees; others won't pay anything—instead, a whole group of individuals will come together but pay out of their own pockets at a discount.

How did you get started in your career?

I taught aerobics while I was in school studying journalism and public relations. I'd always looked up to Dr. Kenneth

Cooper, who was the pioneer in aerobic exercise, often referring to his books and occasionally calling the Cooper Institute if I had questions. I decided I really wanted to go into the corporate fitness area. So one summer I worked at the Cooper Institute as an intern in the public relations department.

Can you tell me about your first job out of school?
I was waitressing and working in a clothing store while looking for a permanent job. Then the executive director at the center needed someone to be a marketing assistant. I entered information into our computer system, gave occasional tours, helped put together promotional fliers. After two months there was an opening for a salesperson at the Fitness Center, and I got the job.

What is a sales rep's day like?
I work from 8 A.M. to 5 P.M. or 10 A.M. to 7 P.M. A lot of what I do depends on how many people come in to check out the club. I do a lot of phone sales to people who may have toured the facility before or who may have requested information in the mail. I give tours regularly, and occasionally I'll visit companies to try to drum up memberships; I handle these corporate accounts once they're established. I also help with promotion.

What's involved in making a sale?
Unlike salespeople at a lot of facilities, we're not real pushy here. That's kind of nice. Basically when someone walks in the door, we give him or her a standard packet of information about the center. Then we'll take them on a tour and explain about our rates; they may or may not sign up right away. We usually give out a couple of guest passes so they can try out the facility. If they don't join then, I'll follow up after a week or two. Sometimes you think you've lost a potential member, and then they pop up six months later.

Are you paid on commission or do you get a salary?
I get a salary as well as a commission. Once you sell a certain number of memberships each month, you start making a percentage on what you sell beyond that. When you sell past a certain dollar mark, you get a bonus and the percentage you earn gets bigger. But there isn't cut-throat competition between sales reps.

What do you enjoy most about your work?

I really like meeting with members and prospective clients.
I do take time to go into the fitness facility and walk
through to talk to people. I think they really appreciate that
people care about them. But for the most part there's not a
whole lot of follow-up after the sale. One thing I think is
really great about working in the industry is that most people are serious about their workout and their health. For the
most part, it's a great, energetic group of people and you
don't have to deal with a lot of flack.

Is there anything you don't enjoy about your job?

Sometimes it's boring to be on the telephone all day. It gets
to where when I get home in the evening, I don't feel like
talking on the phone with friends. We do cold calling (to
businesses or individuals who have not shown interest in
the club so far) to try to sell them on it. Sometimes the
whole sales team from all the different divisions will go
out for two days and drop off information at local companies. Then we have to follow up on that. You may or may
not have left the information with the right person, so this
part of the job is not one of my favorites.

**Do you have to deal with people who are annoyed that
you called?**

For the most part people are nice. We're not forceful. We
take the approach that we're out visiting a neighbor, and
they're generally pretty receptive.

**What have been your best accomplishments as a
salesperson?**

Since I've been here, the number of corporate memberships
has increased 80 percent; it was a mess when I started.
Also, we have a networking breakfast that I host for
members and area businesspeople. We've gotten a few
memberships out of it.

**What are qualities you feel a health club sales rep
should have?**

You have to have a strong desire to be in this field and a
personal interest in fitness and the people who come in.
You also need a big heart because you'll meet people who
are extremely overweight who are seriously looking for
help. We have seniors here who need direction and have

never worked out in their lives. You have to understand that starting an exercise program is a big step for them.

Do you need to know a lot about fitness?
Yes. Even when you're in the sales department of a club, you should have a basic understanding of fitness. People will ask all sorts of questions, and you don't want to give them wrong information.

Do you work out yourself?
Absolutely. If I don't believe in what I'm selling and I don't take my own advice, then I'm not a very good example. It'd be like endorsing a product you don't use.

Dennis Terry, 30,
assistant general manager,
The Houstonian Club,
Houston, Texas
Years in the business: six

How did you break into health club management?
I was working as a fitness director at a health club when I decided to go into sales. I felt there was more money in it and an opportunity to move up eventually into management.

What did you do to pursue that goal?
I was hired as a fitness director at another club. The club decided to start a sales and marketing division. It had never had a sales and marketing person before, so a consultant was called in to help set it up. It sounded so interesting and challenging that I decided it was something I wanted to do—and the club let me.

Had you had previous sales experience?
None whatsoever. But I think my personality and eagerness to sell the idea of fitness to people helped a lot. You have to understand the industry to sell memberships and be able to explain the benefits that you get when you belong to a club—which is what you have to do when you're on the floor, too.

What was the hardest aspect of your job in the beginning?
Being comfortable with being rejected—and I wasn't at first. I took it personally when people didn't join. It took me three or four months to get past that. I finally realized that you have to give people the opportunity to say "No." I was trying to overcome every objection they had to joining, to the point that it made them feel uncomfortable turning me down.

How long did it take you to get established?
I took on a whole team of salespeople right away and learned the job as I went, which isn't typical. Membership sales is an ongoing process. Commonly in health clubs 80 to 90 percent of all new memberships come from current members. When you start selling, you get a lot of leads and more sales from people you sold to before. It took me six months to sell 100 memberships. After that a lot of my sales came from referrals.

How many people work under you now?
About 100. As an assistant general manager, I'm in charge of the club's operations manager, food and beverage operations, locker room attendants, laundry service, housekeeping, membership check-in and the retail sales pro shop. We have three salespeople, but we have a sales manager who oversees them. Now I do outside sales consulting with other health clubs, helping them set up their sales and marketing programs, hiring people and training staff.

What do you like most about what you're doing?
The consulting with outside clubs—helping them get their systems in place. It's fun to walk in and be the expert. I also like the responsibility of being in charge of the people who actually interact with the members, because they will make or break the success of the club. I enjoy being able to motivate them.

What do you like least about your work?
It can be difficult to make every member happy, which is the ultimate goal—especially in a club like ours that has so many features. You just can't please everyone.

What advice would you give to someone thinking of entering this field?

Personality means so much. If you can sell yourself to a member, you can sell the club. The most successful people feel confident about themselves. You have to be a good communicator—able to walk into a party and strike up a conversation with anyone. You have to be fit yourself, live what you sell. People won't buy memberships from sales people who are overweight or smoke.

Floor staff are like lifeguards: They keep watch over a roomful of moving bodies all at once, on the lookout for the novice who is performing an exercise in a dangerous manner, the health club hog who is monopolizing the machines and the regular member who is ready for an updated routine. Their job is to help people exercise safely and effectively.

To do this they must understand how muscles move and how the body responds to different types of activity. Floor staff (they're sometimes called exercise trainers or fitness instructors) must know how to use various types of exercise machines and weight-training equipment and be able to teach others how to use them.

Floor staff sometimes work with individuals. They show newcomers how to use each piece of equipment and

71

develop fitness programs based on personal goals and limitations. In some fitness facilities staffers may spend time as personal trainers, working one-on-one with individuals, or teach exercise classes. Health clubs may also require floor staff to help sell memberships to prospective clients; in larger clubs this job is set aside for member or sales representatives. Health clubs with few employees may put floor staff to work keeping the equipment clean and the locker rooms tidy.

Most floor staff do not mind these extra duties because their job allows them to stay close to something they love: exercise. They practice what they preach by keeping in tip-top shape—and this is easily done, as one of the perks of health club employment is full use of the facilities on days off. In fact, it is important that a health club employee look the part: Who would trust an overweight weakling to teach exercise? On the other hand, good floor staff are not so self-absorbed that they cannot focus completely on others.

If you enjoy exercise, are intrigued by the ways physical fitness can benefit the body, have a knack for showing others how to exercise and can keep your mind on more than one thing at a time, then you should feel right at home in a health club or other facility that has a fitness program, such as a YMCA. You may start out working only part time, but if you do your job well, keep up with new trends and take continuing education workshops, then you may progress steadily up the not-so-corporate ladder of the health club world.

What You Need to Know

- ❏ Anatomy (where bones, muscles and joints are located and how they work together)
- ❏ The effects different types of exercise (cardiovascular, strength training, stretching) have on the body
- ❏ How to design safe, effective and well-rounded exercise programs for individuals with different needs
- ❏ How fitness equipment works (cardiovascular machines, strength training machines, free weights)
- ❏ Sports medicine basics (enough to recognize a minor injury and be able to recommend the proper specialist for treatment)
- ❏ Very basic nutrition (how foods affect weight loss and gain, which foods deliver energy, basic good eating habits)

Necessary Skills

- ❏ Ability to spot a client who is lifting weights (make sure moves are performed correctly and safely, and when necessary, assist with lifting a weight)
- ❏ Ability to talk about abstract concepts, such as how a muscle should feel as it is moved a certain way
- ❏ An eye for judging correct exercise form in other people
- ❏ Ability to solve problems (being able to find new approaches to fitness when an old routine isn't working)

Do You Have What It Takes?

- ❏ Diplomacy (knowing how to settle disagreements between exercisers and not put people off)
- ❏ An interest in helping others improve their image—physically and mentally
- ❏ A nurturing personality
- ❏ Patience
- ❏ A thick skin (not getting bent out of shape when members complain or criticize your advice)

◆ **Getting into the Field**

Physical Attributes

❑ Good physical condition—looking visibly fit
❑ Nonsmoker
❑ Well-groomed appearance (good personal hygiene is critical because close physical contact with others is unavoidable on the fitness floor)

Education

A high school diploma is preferred. An associate degree in a fitness field is a plus. Health club clientele are becoming more and more sophisticated about health and fitness, and so they expect those who instruct them to be equally knowledgeable.

Licenses Required

All health club employees must be certified in CPR (cardiopulmonary resuscitation, a set of skills used when someone has stopped breathing or his or her heart has stopped). Many clubs require employees who will be working directly with exercisers to be certified in fitness training.

Job Outlook

Competition for jobs: somewhat competitive

Fitness has become a lifestyle for many people, which means health clubs and other exercise centers will continue to prosper and take on new employees. But job applicants who have no formal training in anatomy, exercise physiology and fitness may find themselves edged out by people who do. The good news: most health club managers admit that they can be as impressed by a talent for teaching and a practical understanding of the rudiments of fitness as they can by a college degree.

The Ground Floor

Entry-level job: floor staff

Chances are this may be a part-time position at first, but as you gain experience and expertise, you will be able to add hours and responsibilities.

Beginners

- ❑ Teach new club members how to use equipment
- ❑ Set up basic fitness programs for clients; update them as needed
- ❑ Make sure club members exercise and use equipment safely and correctly
- ❑ Inspect equipment frequently to make sure it is in good working order
- ❑ Sell club memberships (in some places)
- ❑ Coach one-on-one training sessions (in some places)
- ❑ Help keep exercise area and locker rooms clean

Shift Supervisors

In addition to the above:
- ❑ Oversee the staff working during the shift (making sure there are enough instructors on hand and that they are doing their jobs)
- ❑ Have the final word when members challenge rules and regulations
- ❑ Decide when a machine should be put out of order

Floor Supervisors

In addition to the above:
- ❑ Interview and sometimes hire new staff
- ❑ Evaluate how well instructors do their jobs
- ❑ Design special programs, competitions and work- shops for members

(Note: Fitness facilities vary widely in employee re- sponsibilities and job progression; the job descriptions above are some of the many possibilities.)

Most fitness facilities are open seven days a week for at least 16 hours per day. Entry-level staffers often start by working part-time hours; with experience, they get more hours and eventually will work at least 40 hours a week, with possible overtime. Most floor staff are required to put in some weekend hours.

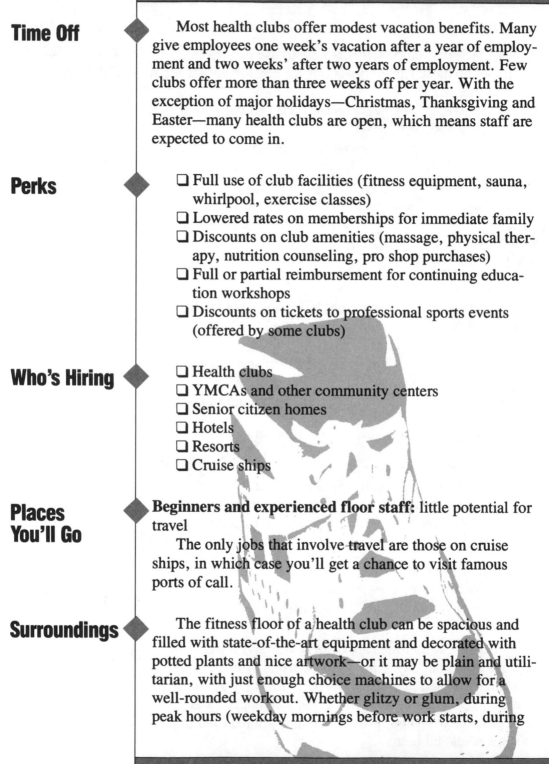

Time Off

Most health clubs offer modest vacation benefits. Many give employees one week's vacation after a year of employment and two weeks' after two years of employment. Few clubs offer more than three weeks off per year. With the exception of major holidays—Christmas, Thanksgiving and Easter—many health clubs are open, which means staff are expected to come in.

Perks

❏ Full use of club facilities (fitness equipment, sauna, whirlpool, exercise classes)
❏ Lowered rates on memberships for immediate family
❏ Discounts on club amenities (massage, physical therapy, nutrition counseling, pro shop purchases)
❏ Full or partial reimbursement for continuing education workshops
❏ Discounts on tickets to professional sports events (offered by some clubs)

Who's Hiring

❏ Health clubs
❏ YMCAs and other community centers
❏ Senior citizen homes
❏ Hotels
❏ Resorts
❏ Cruise ships

Places You'll Go

Beginners and experienced floor staff: little potential for travel

The only jobs that involve travel are those on cruise ships, in which case you'll get a chance to visit famous ports of call.

Surroundings

The fitness floor of a health club can be spacious and filled with state-of-the-art equipment and decorated with potted plants and nice artwork—or it may be plain and utilitarian, with just enough choice machines to allow for a well-rounded workout. Whether glitzy or glum, during peak hours (weekday mornings before work starts, during lunch hour, right after the end of the typical eight-hour day, on weekends) health clubs throb with activity; other times they may be almost empty.

◆ **Dollars and Cents**

Beginners, particularly those who start out as part-time employees, generally earn the minimum hourly wage. Full-time staffers in metropolitan areas average about $6 to $8 per hour, while those working in suburban locales pocket slightly less—$5 to $6 per hour. Those who work their way up to become staff supervisors may pull in as much as $18,000 to $27,000 per year. For employees who draw an hourly wage, overtime pay is frequently offered, usually at a rate of time-and-a-half. Health club staffers who also sell memberships may earn a small commission.

◆ **Moving Up**

Getting a promotion depends on how well you perform: Are you attentive to club members and always available to answer questions? Do you make an effort to remember exercisers' names and their fitness likes and dislikes? Do you keep an eye out for faulty equipment and tidy up the floor frequently? Doing your job well will earn you the points that lead to promotion—so will keeping up with new fitness trends by reading journals and other related material, attending local lectures and workshops and updating any certifications you have.

◆ **Where the Jobs Are**

Most fitness centers are clustered in large metropolitan areas and surrounding suburbs, but they can be found throughout the United States, even in small towns. There are also more than 2,000 YMCAs throughout the country with various types of fitness programs.

◆ **Training**

There are dozens of small certification programs and workshops run by professional and industry associations. Two of the most widely recognized are: the American Council on Exercise (ACE) and the Aerobics and Fitness Association of America (AFAA). Both offer workshops in the basics of anatomy, kinesiology (how the body moves), exercise physiology and other fitness subjects.

The Male/Female Equation

Neither sex dominates in the population of fitness instructors.

Making a Decision: What to Consider

The Bad News

❏ Promotions may be few and far between
❏ Most clubs are open on weekends and holidays
❏ Club members may be difficult and temperamental
❏ Low starting pay
❏ Duties may include tidying up exercise area and locker rooms

The Good News

❏ Fitness facilities are open to off-duty staff
❏ Different shifts are available, allowing flexible scheduling
❏ The opportunity to help people become stronger and healthier
❏ Salaries may rise substantially with promotions
❏ Some clubs offer commission for selling memberships

WHAT IT'S REALLY LIKE

Paula Ames, 25, fitness instructor,
Gainesville Health and Fitness Club,
Gainesville, Florida
Years in the business: one

What led you to become a fitness instructor?
I have always wanted to be a physical education teacher
and was going to school part time while working as a secretary at a community college. I wound up quitting school
because it was expensive, but then I landed this job as a
fitness instructor.

What sort of experience did you have?
I did gymnastics when I was younger, and I was certified
to be an aerobics teacher. I also worked out in the weight
room at the college where I had been a secretary. But I had
no actual experience as a floor instructor. My club, however, has a very strong training program.

Could you describe the training?
It lasted a total of about 20 hours. During the first two sessions I learned about anatomy and how to instruct people
on the Nautilus machines. The last two sessions I took part
in were what we call the shadow team: First I "shadowed"

an experienced instructor, following her around to see how to organize a workout, motivate members and so forth. Later I was shadowed while I worked with someone. At the same time, the shadower asked me questions about fitness, anatomy, the machines. After the training I felt ready to go out on the floor and work with members on my own.

What was the most difficult part of the training?
Being followed by the shadow team person. Even though I knew the information, it was scary to be out there having someone quizzing me on everything I did.

What do you do now?
Besides being a Nautilus instructor, I'm the coordinator of our Nautilus diet and exercise program: It's a six-week program in which I help people learn about exercise and how to lose weight by changing their eating habits. The people who sign up for this program have a one-on-one trainer who takes them through a high-intensity workout three times a week. I work as a personal trainer for those people, and I'm also on the shadow team, which means I have to know more than the regular instructors.

Do you have any other responsibilities?
Occasionally I give seminars to club members on specific fitness topics. Recently I did pregnancy and exercise. Sometimes we trade off—one instructor may do the research, another may present the seminar.

How long did it take before you took on those responsibilities?
Six or seven months. First I came onto the shadow team; after that I became a diet instructor. The club's diet coordinator usually interviews the Nautilus instructors with the best motivational skills to become diet instructors.

What are your hours like?
It's close to full time. I work on the floor three days a week: one three-hour shift, then one five-hour shift each day. I also work with Nautilus diet people in between shifts—how often depends on how many people sign up. I've had as many as four people in a six-week program.

What do you like most about your work?
I enjoy it all. I like being on the shadow team because I can
help other instructors learn more. With the diet program
it's a personal achievement to help members reach their
goals, to see their weight go down or their body fat percentage change for the better.

Is there anything you don't like about the job?
There's some potential for getting frustrated, say, when a
member can't use a certain machine for medical reasons.
But then it's challenging to find other ways to work with
someone like that. You get to be creative.

What are your greatest achievements so far?
I'm proud that I've progressed so quickly. It's also very
satisfying when members ask for me or refer me to other
people and say I'm the best. One girl told me recently, "I
want to take you home with me, you've helped me so
much." Sometimes they call me the instructor from hell
because I'm not afraid to really push people to work hard.

Jim Modlin, 44, health club manager, Fitness Today, Greensboro, North Carolina
Years in the business: three

How did you break into the field?
I had been selling jewelry wholesale and traveling a lot
when I joined this health club. I became friends with the
owner of the club, who asked me if I'd be interested in a
job. At the same time, I had gotten married and wanted to
quit traveling so much.

Describe your first job.
I was a part-time fitness consultant. I worked 20 hours a
week, setting up exercise programs, selling memberships,
maintaining equipment—a little bit of everything. Eventually I started screening people to be hired.

Was it a "usual" first job?
Yes. At most places it is hard to go in and be full time immediately. Having never actually been involved in the busi-

ness, this was a nice transition for me: I didn't know if it would work out as a profession.

What kind of preparation did you have?
When I traveled, I worked out at different health clubs. I learned about different types of exercises, equipment and systems. That information helped me when I started, although I had to get up to speed on how things were done here. The manager led me through that. I don't yet have my personal trainer certification, but I was CPR-certified when I started.

What was the hardest aspect of working in this field at first?
Changing something I used to do for fun into something I had to do eight to ten hours a day. All of a sudden my hobby was gone. It wasn't a change for the worse, just a change.

How long did it take you to get established?
About a year. It was a natural fit and I know I'm good at it.

How many different jobs have you held in this field?
After coming on as a full-time staff person, I was promoted to assistant manager and then manager.

What do you currently do?
I'm in charge of personnel—hiring, training and scheduling staff members. I also sell club memberships and set new members up on training programs. Then there's the business end: Doing the books, making deposits, getting people in to maintain equipment, paying bills. You end up being a jack-of-all-trades. The only aspect of the club I don't have anything to do with is the aerobics program.

What do you like most about your work?
Helping people enjoy exercise and get results. I've seen people who are 150 pounds overweight: To see them change completely makes me feel good. I also like the sales part of my job.

What do you like least?
Dealing with customers you can't satisfy, who always have something to complain about. Some people can't understand why a broken piece of equipment can't be fixed immediately, but they are a distinct minority.

What have your proudest achievements been?
For one thing, our club is making money, which is something I can document on paper. And people compliment me day to day on how good the club looks, say thank you for helping them with some machine—that kind of feedback makes me feel good. A health club is like a baby; it's really a hands-on business. I'm proud to be able to keep it all in working order.

What advice would you give to someone who is thinking about working in a health club?
Enjoy the physical end of it first. Then realize there is a business aspect to it and get some experience by helping to manage a recreation facility in the summertime or by working in a sporting goods store.

Skip Tull, 47, Nautilus supervisor,
South Shore YMCA,
Quincy, Massachusetts
Years in the business: eight

How did you break into the field?
When my dad came down with Alzheimer's, I began taking him to the Y; I was a musician at the time. While he was working out with friends, I worked out at the Nautilus center. I started asking questions of the best instructors; they were my first teachers. I also read up on how to get a more effective workout for myself. As I became more knowledgeable I started to assist other people with their workouts. One day the fitness director came into the center while I was working with one of the newer instructors on proper technique. She said, ''You should work for us,'' and I said, ''Put me on the payroll.''

Describe your first job and what you did on it.
I worked as a substitute Nautilus instructor, so I was ''on call.'' I would work two or three hours a week in the beginning. When new members came in, I would show them how to use the Nautilus equipment. Then I would teach them how to do some form of aerobic exercise and how to monitor their heart rate.

I also started working with older members, helping them to revise their workouts. That wasn't part of the job, just something I started doing.

Was it a "usual" first job?
We've hired other people that way before. We call them as we need them, and if they show dedication and consistency, we'll often hire them when a job opens up.

What kind of preparation did you have?
A lot of it was reading books and asking questions of everybody who seemed to know something about fitness. Often I would end up with half a dozen varying opinions and techniques and through trial and error find what was most effective. After I went on the payroll, I earned my YMCA strength training certification, which involved taking a two-day workshop and then an exam.

What was the hardest aspect of working in this field during your first few years?
Getting people who had been working out ineffectively for many years to be open to new training techniques. Often they needed to watch me work with other people for a long time before they would be open to change or suggestions. Now I train a lot of the instructors, so that's given me credibility in the members' eyes.

How long did it take you to get established?
I've been in this position now for about two years. It took about four months to go from substitute to scheduled position, then about five years to move up.

How many different jobs have you held in this field?
Three: from substitute instructor to staffer, and from staffer right to supervisor.

What do you currently do?
Mostly I supervise the staff and train new instructors. Four nights a week I give a slide show orientation for all new Y members who join the Nautilus center. I also train children ages 9 to 14 in a youth fitness program to use Nautilus machines and I work with paraplegics and quadriplegics.

The Y allows me to use their facilities to train private clients one-on-one; part of the deal is I don't cut back on my regular schedule. I train some private clients in their homes.

What do you most like about your work?

I love getting new members directed toward realistic fitness goals. A lot of people come in not really knowing what's effective and available. Sometimes what they are trying to achieve is not physiologically or metabolically possible. If I can get them to see what is possible for them and show them what they need to do to achieve those goals, then they have a really good opportunity to have a positive experience.

What do you least like about your work?

Except for my private work, the pay. But that's okay. I don't like to have to be a policeman and deal with unpleasant situations between members. There's a real problem with men taking advantage of women by monopolizing the machines. There can be some tension and you have to be a real diplomat to diffuse it.

What have your proudest achievements been?

I gave a strength training presentation as part of an all-day workshop for coaches for the Special Olympics. I've also been working on their fitness manual and setting up a workshop to bring their coaches in to train them in our center.

What advice would you give to someone who was thinking of going into this field?

Certification is great, but you may also want to find a good, successful trainer and offer to work as an intern in order to learn the business. Once you know your stuff, look for a need in a fitness facility, something that isn't presently there, and offer to fulfill it.

MORE INFORMATION PLEASE

American Council on Exercise
P.O. Box 910449
San Diego, California 92191-0449
619-452-1ACE

This is a certifying organization for group exercise instructors and personal trainers. It offers workshops, study materials and certification exams for both new instructors and those wishing to update their credentials. ACE also sponsors continuing education courses.

Aerobics and Fitness Association of America (AFAA)
15250 Ventura Blvd., Suite 310
Sherman Oaks, California 91403-3297
800-446-AFAA
800-225-2322 (Canada and Mexico)

In addition to a primary certification in exercise instruction, AFAA offers workshops in teaching special populations (pregnant women, seniors, the overweight) and has a certification program for personal trainers. Members receive travel discounts and *American Fitness* magazine and are eligible for liability insurance coverage as well as personal health insurance benefits.

Aquatic Exercise Association
P.O. Box 497
Port Washington, Wisconsin 53074
414-284-3416

This group offers a one-day review of basic water exercise principles, followed by a certification exam.

IDEA: The Association for Fitness Professionals
6190 Cornerstone Court East, Suite 204
San Diego, California 92121-0449
800-999-4332
619-535-8979

A professional organization for fitness instructors, group exercise teachers and personal trainers. Membership includes a subscription to *Idea Today*, a magazine that features education articles, industry news, job openings worldwide and notices of local workshops, as well as product and travel discounts and eligibility for liability insurance. IDEA holds several conventions for members throughout the year, at which certification exams may be given.

Cooper Institute for Aerobics Research
12330 Preston Road
Dallas, Texas 75230
800-635-7050
214-701-6875

Founded by fitness authority Kenneth Cooper, M.D., this organization offers four levels of certification. Participants travel to Dallas for a five-day training workshop, at the end of which there is a written and a practical exam. Workshops are given once a month. CPR certification is required.

Jazzercise, Inc.
International Headquarters
2808 Roosevelt Street
Carlsbad, California 92008
619-434-2101

Jazzercise provides information on purchasing a franchise, helps locate studio space and gives instruction workshops and certification exams.

United States Water Fitness Association
P.O. Box 3279
Boynton Beach, Florida 33424
407-732-9908

This association has two certification programs, one for water fitness instructors and another for people interested in coordinating a water fitness program at a pool, health club or other facility.

WILL YOU FIT INTO THE WORLD OF FITNESS?

Before you enroll in a training program or start to search for a job in one of the careers described in this book, it's smart to figure out whether that career is a good fit, given your background, skills and personality. There are a number of ways to do that. They include:

❑ Talk to people who work in that field. Find out what they like and don't like about their jobs, what kinds of people their employers hire and what their recommendations are about training.

❑ Use a computer to help you identify career options. Some of the most widely used programs are "Discover," by the American College Testing Service, "SIGI Plus," developed by the Educational Testing Service, and "Career Options," by Peterson's. Some public libraries make this career software available to library users at low or no cost. The career counseling or guidance office of your high school or local community college is another possibility.

❑ Take a vocational interest test. The most commonly used ones are the Strong-Campbell Interest Inventory and the Kuder Occupational Interest Survey. High schools and colleges usually offer free testing to their students and alumni through their guidance and career-planning offices. Many career counselors in private practice or at community job centers are also trained to interpret results.

❑ Talk to a career counselor. You can find one by asking friends and colleagues if they know of any good ones. Or contact the career information office of the adult education division of a local college. Its staff and workshop leaders often do one-on-one counseling. The job information services division of major libraries sometimes offer low- or no-cost counseling by appointment. Or check the *Yellow Pages* under the heading "Vocational Guidance."

Before you spend time, energy or money doing any of the above, take one or more of the following five quizzes (one for each career described in the book). The results can help you confirm whether you really are cut out to work in a particular career.

If becoming a group exercise instructor interests you, take this quiz:

Read each statement, then choose the number 0, 5 or 10. The rating scale below explains what each number means.

> **0** = Disagree
> **5** = Agree somewhat
> **10** = Strongly agree

____I am coordinated and have a good sense of rhythm

____I know which exercise moves are safe and which can
 • cause injuries

____I have the ability to break down dance steps into easy-to-follow segments

____I know how to choreograph a dance routine

____I have an enthusiastic, motivating personality

____I know how to give exercisers well-timed directions for changes in steps

____I can do more than one thing at a time—that is, watch a large group of people while leading a class

____I am not shy about leading exercises in front of other people

____I can motivate and lead others

___I am in good physical condition and have plenty of stamina

Now add up your score.   ___Total points

If your total points were less than 50, you probably do not have sufficient interest or inclination to learn what's required to teach exercise classes. If your total points were between 50 and 75, you may have what it takes to lead a class, but you should do more investigation by taking classes yourself, talking with instructors and reading up on anatomy and exercise principles before taking the plunge. If you scored above 75 points, you are probably cut out to be a group exercise instructor and will want to explore the training and certification process.

If you are interested in becoming a personal trainer, take this quiz:

Read each statement, then choose the number 0, 5 or 10. The rating scale below explains what each number means.

0 = Disagree
5 = Agree somewhat
10 = Strongly agree

___I understand how exercise benefits the body physically and mentally

___I know how to achieve aerobic fitness, muscle strength and flexibility with exercise

___I know or would like to learn how to evaluate a person's fitness level

___I like the idea of being self-employed

___I can explain to others how to use exercise machines, lift weights and perform other tasks involved in training

___I am able to tell when a person is performing an exercise incorrectly and to correct them in a way that will not offend

___I can put together a complete exercise program with little or no equipment

___I am patient and tactful with people I am teaching

___I have the ability to take charge of exercise sessions firmly and diplomatically without being bossy

___I can deal with having unusual or irregular work hours

Now add up your score.   ___Total points

If your total points were less than 50, you probably do not have enough interest or determination to become a personal trainer. If your total points were between 50 and 75, you may have what it takes to help others work out on a one-on-one basis, but it would help you to learn more by working with a trainer yourself and attending some lectures or workshops on personal training. If you scored above 75 points, a career in personal training is within your grasp.

If health club sales and service work interests you, take this quiz:

Read each statement, then choose the number 0, 5 or 10. The rating scale below explains what each number means.

0 = Disagree
5 = Agree somewhat
10 = Strongly agree

___I have a basic understanding of fitness: how exercise affects the body and how different machines and training methods work

___I enjoy keeping up with developments in the fitness industry

___I stay in shape myself

___I have good one-on-one communication skills

___I have enough business sense to be able to understand the terms of a contract and explain it to others

___I am able to handle money and simple business transactions

___I have good phone etiquette

___I am comfortable meeting and speaking with strangers

___I have a knack for salesmanship and can handle rejection

___I enjoy being of service to other people and don't mind solving complaints

Now add up your score.   ___Total points

If your total points were less than 50, you probably are not cut out to work in the business end of a health club. If you scored between 50 and 75 points, you may have suffic-ient interest in health club sales and service work, but you may want to check out this career further—by talking with people in the field, for instance. If your points were above 75, consider yourself a prime candidate for a job selling health club memberships, running the reception desk or performing a similar job.

If sports massage therapy interests you, take this quiz:

Read each statement, then choose the number 0, 5 or 10. The rating scale below explains what each number means.

> **0** = Disagree
> **5** = Agree somewhat
> **10** = Strongly agree

___I know or would like to learn basic anatomy

___I know or would like to learn the basic massage strokes

___I know or would like to learn fundamental first aid

___I have mastered enough simple business skills to keep financial records, promote myself, etc.

___I am good with my hands and have a keen sense of "feel"

___I am a good listener

___I am interested in sports and exercise myself

___I have a desire to help heal

___I have an interest in being part of an athlete's care and training

___I would like to be self-employed

Now add up your score.   ___Total points

If you scored less than 50, you probably are not interested enough in sports massage therapy to make a successful go of it. If your total points were between 50 and 75, you may have a knack for massage and enough knowledge about the body to get started, but you should investigate the career further by talking with established therapists. If your score was above 75 points, you definitely have what it takes to pursue a career in sports massage therapy.

If becoming a fitness floor staffer interests you, take this quiz:

Read each statement, then choose the number 0, 5 or 10. The rating scale below explains what each number means.

0 = Disagree
5 = Agree somewhat
10 = Strongly agree

___I want to help others improve their image—physically and mentally

___I am familiar with a variety of exercise machines and training techniques

___I have the ability to talk about abstract concepts, such as how a muscle should feel as it is moved a certain way

___I have an eye for judging exercise form in other people and have a knack for correcting faulty form in a way that does not offend people

___I can "spot," that is, make sure moves are performed correctly and safely and, when necessary, assist with lifting a weight

___I have an interest in helping others get the best out of their workouts and improving their image

___I am a patient teacher

___I am diplomatic; I could settle disagreements between exercisers and not put people off

___I can keep an eye on more than one person at a time

___I can handle criticism or complaints from others without taking it personally

Now add up your score.   ___Total points

If your score was less than 50 points, you probably do not have enough interest in becoming a fitness instructor to learn what is necessary. If your total points were between 50 and 75, you may have what it takes to become a fitness instructor, but be sure to investigate further, perhaps by talking with the instructors in your club about their backgrounds and duties. If you scored above 75 points, a career as a health club fitness trainer is right up your alley and you should be able to easily handle the training and education that's involved.

ABOUT THE
AUTHOR

Maura Rhodes Curless is a freelance writer and editor who lives in Scarsdale, New York. Her work has appeared in such publications as *Self*, *Longevity*, *McCall's* and *Redbook*. She was formerly senior fitness editor of *Health* magazine. In ten years of covering the fitness industry, she has reported on fitness firsthand from a dude range in the Catskills, to a spa in Brazil, to classes at some of the hottest studios in Manhattan.